THE
OKANAGAN
TABLE

THE ART OF EVERYDAY
HOME COOKING

THE OKANAGAN TABLE

ROD BUTTERS

with Kerry Gold

Figure 1
Vancouver / Berkeley

SUNRISE

MIDDAY

SUNSET

TWILIGHT

CONTENTS

CHALLENGE YOUR LIMITS, DO NOT LIMIT YOUR CHALLENGES

BY *Bernard Casavant*

I MET ROD IN 1987 when I joined the Four Seasons Vancouver as executive sous chef. Rod was chef de partie at the time, and we worked together in the banquet kitchen. At one function, I asked him if he knew how to cook wild rice. He explained that he cooked it to just the bursting stage and no more. Right then and there, I knew that we would be cooking very well together. Although wild rice is simple to cook, it has to be exactly right, something most cooks at the time did not focus on. This was a tiny glimpse into his style, and why he has been so successful in his career. In 1989, we moved to Whistler to launch the Chateau Whistler Resort. With Rod as executive sous chef, we opened this magnificent property redefining the CP hotel dining standard and the CP Hotel Apprenticeship program. Our opening team comprised numerous cooks who are today industry-leading chefs all over Canada and the world. For such a remote location, very impressive.

Over the years our friendship has endured. As chefs, we maintain many similar values and continue to cook together at various events. He's collaborative and solutions-minded, and he isn't afraid to tell you when he disagrees. He comes across as steely, intense, and resilient, and he is the most compassionate and biggest man I know.

He operates in his kitchen with an iron fist — serious, ordered, focused, and disciplined — but he's also the first to mark birthdays and anniversaries, and the person to be the drive behind any group funding for worthy causes. As best friends, we both like our privacy, but whenever we get together at one of our homes, we simply "cook." What's fresh, what's local, what will create a food memory?

Few people realize what it means to be a cook or chef. A cook works to a chef's standards. A chef sets the standards for the cooks to work to. And we all cook for a living. Rod can cook, a real grounded, rooted style, and he stands independent amongst other cooks. He proudly takes on the challenge of being local and requires his team to understand and embrace that philosophy. One of the many quotes he has posted at the restaurant, "Challenge your limits, do not limit your challenges," truly describes him.

This cookbook is intended to serve the home cook. It was a challenge indeed for Rod to compose recipes for limited quantities after a lifetime of working in professional kitchens, but he has done an amazing job. The recipes in this book are honest, locally rooted, and absolutely delicious. I'm very proud of my friend Chef Butters, for putting so much effort into this project. What took so long?

A CHEF'S PLAYGROUND

BY *Anita Stewart, C.M. LL.D.*

WHAT CHEF ROD BUTTERS has chronicled over the years — and what his diners have so generously responded to — are menus that reflect our community and collective culture... on a plate. He has provided us all with an authentic glimpse into the here and now that we all recognize as Canada: multi-layered, multi-ethnic, innovative, and profoundly regional. His recipes demonstrate an utter commitment to the food of the Okanagan Valley, both cultivated and foraged. They also tell a story of a unique culinary calling.

To contextualize Rod's career within Canadian cuisine demands that we remember the times in which he was growing and working between the late 1970s and the 1990s. It's only through this lens that we can see just how impressive his contribution has been. His is a magnificent and inspirational story. While thousands of chefs are now on the local food bandwagon, only a few were present when the wheels were affixed — and Rod Butters was one of them. These were the decades in our culinary history when the more exotic the ingredient was and the further it had travelled from some obscure corner of the planet, the more it was valued.

While Rod was learning to execute the most delicious preparations at Toronto's splendid Scaramouche, a restaurant that is still on the forefront of dining excellence in that city, the notion of local procurement was just beginning to take shape in British Columbia. When Rod arrived in B.C. just after Expo 86, Vancouver was becoming a force on the national stage, yet food was still largely from away. With *The Official Cookbook of Expo 86*, author Susan Mendelson honoured the city's great restaurateurs (of whom there were many), and nary a local supplier was mentioned. The word "gourmet" was being bandied about, yet Vancouver Island salt, Salt Spring Island mussels, and Cortes Island cultured oysters were nonexistent. And B.C. spot prawns, now prized by chefs across Canada, were safely flitting about in their watery homes in the Strait of Georgia. The Vintners Quality Alliance (VQA) had yet to arrive to B.C.'s nascent wine regions, and Pemberton was still a small town where there were few potato patches to speak of and, more importantly, no good vodka. Brewpubs were just starting — the oldest, Spinnakers in Victoria, was founded in 1984 — and any micro-distillery was of the illegal sort. The concept of Pacific Northwest cuisine was being explored, but only one Vancouver Island restaurant, Sooke Harbour House, walked that talk authentically.

So imagine the utter bravado and daring of this young man, to imagine a locally sourced menu into being at a brand new, oceanside resort in a tiny village isolated by dense rainforest on one side and pounding surf on the other. Landing in Tofino as he did, with his creativity and chutzpah completely intact, he proceeded to put the Pointe Restaurant at the Wickaninnish Inn on Canada's culinary map. With the support of the inordinately proud owners, the McDiarmid family, the Wick was awarded membership in Relais & Châteaux within a year of its inception—a feat that had never occurred prior to that time and, to my knowledge, has not happened since.

Great chefs are at once botanists and bookkeepers, recipe developers and cultural commentators. They are purveyors of nutrition and pleasure providers. Great chefs possess common traits: huge stamina, organizational skills, well-developed taste buds, and curiosity! And it was this curiosity that spurred Rod on to Kelowna, where he and business partner Audrey Surrao formed the backbone of a new era

of dining. Their great friend Bernard Casavant soon followed, and as a result, the city blossomed into the culinary heart of one of the most dynamic gastronomic regions in North America. Rod Butters is a game changer, a pioneer, and an innovator. With this book, he is helping us all cook a better future. Stay tuned... knowing Rod, there's likely a lot more to come!

WHY HE COOKS

BY *Jamie Maw*

ROD BUTTERS — now there's a name for a chef!

And fittingly, it describes both the man *and* the cook. If his given name speaks to the steel of his discipline, honed in some of the province's finest kitchens, his surname calls out a softer side, one that has worked tirelessly with local producers and winemakers while listening thoughtfully to the desires of his loyal clientele.

He's greying a little around the temples now, and he's had four knee surgeries. But tonight at his flagship restaurant in downtown Kelowna— RauDZ Regional Table—as the ritual of the nightly slam begins, Butters takes his place on the kitchen line. His smile is bright, knowing, amused—it might even carry a glint of the stoic. He steps up alongside his brigade, expediting Executive Chef Brock Bowes's fast-flying plates. Few words have been exchanged in this silent ballet. Tonight, it seems, the master has become the understudy.

The irony is not lost on me, for during his lengthy career, this is a chef who has trained several hundred protégés. If not all of them survived the rigours of a professional kitchen, it wasn't because their mentor hadn't tried to push them past the flames, and flame-outs— Chef Bowes is one of many exceptions who

prove the rule. I've followed Rod's career for the past three decades, from downtown Vancouver to Tofino and then on to Kelowna at the turn of the millennium, where Rod and co-owner Audrey Surrao's Fresco Restaurant & Lounge turned the Okanagan's dining landscape on its head.

As a food writer, and erstwhile critic, let me tell you that there is no praise higher than saying a chef "cooks clean." Although it's nasty grammar, it means a few things: getting face to face (and down and dirty) with the people who nurture prime ingredients on and in nearby farms, ranches, lakes, and oceans. And then knowing precisely when to get out of the way of that produce—in the grounded patois of this valley, to let those spanking ingredients speak frankly, and often very simply, for themselves. For, and here's Rod's abiding mantra, "The plate should mean complexity without complication, and never—heaven forbid—the reverse." He also holds a healthy disdain for the hackneyed term "farm-to-table," saying, "Of course it is, and it has been forever in the Okanagan—at first out of necessity, now out of choice."

The accolades have poured down on Rod— some being what his more sardonic side might call "one-foot-in-the-grave" accolades, including inductions into the B.C. Restaurant Hall of Fame and the Canadian Culinary Federation Honour Society, and an Okanagan College Honorary Fellow Award. And while he has graciously accepted them, amongst many other plaudits, those who know him best also know that for this cook, glory is best viewed on a clean white plate, or the face of a satisfied customer whose day has been uplifted, maybe even transformed. Or it might come from his massive involvement in the Okanagan Chefs Association — the leadership that he has provided, with other key chefs, has made it one of the most vigorous collaborations (and nurturers of emergent chefs) in the country.

By the 1990s, Kelowna dining had misplaced its local provenance and had gotten lazy: a big night out might have meant a "baseball sirloin" at the Keg, some Icelandic scampi at the Vintage Room, or a buffeteria of unknown Asian sweet-and-sour origin. And in the nether regions of "fine dining," largely found in hotel restaurants of the day, well those chefs were from far away too.

With Fresco, Rod and Audrey brought back the sense of Okanagan locality — and then some. If 2001 was hardly an auspicious year to open a fine-dining restaurant (American tourism fell off a cliff), local wines were still finding their feet in the local soil too. After all, it had been just 13 years since the Great Pull-Out promulgated by the Free Trade Agreement, and true viniferas were still finding their roots. Stubbornly, Rod sought out local wineries for pride of placement on his growing wine list.

He's prescient in other ways, too. When he saw a market in "casual fine dining," he and Audrey threw out the tablecloths and anything fancy and transformed Fresco into RauDZ, a restaurant that was more accessible and just plain fun. The lively bar, enormous communal table, and local artwork fairly shouted "Okanagan!" A few years later they would open their delightful micro bar • bites. Revenues trebled. Soon, he was able to hire more local staff and buy more local produce.

Courage is being afraid of what you really want to do, then doing it. And risk, especially in the restaurant business, is fraught with the sleepless nights that accompany stale-dating product, unwilling bankers, and customers who stay too late at the RauDZ bar, or who don't show up on time — or even at all.

Rod Butters has walked that line with the same amused, stoic smile for more than 30 years, and we are much the better for him.

FOR PEOPLE WHO LOVE TO COOK

AT ITS HEART, this book is about my passionate relationship to food. I've loved cooking my entire life, whether it was making pancakes in my family's kitchen as a kid, or starting out as the lead broiler cook at a chain restaurant. I've been happy in my role as chef de cuisine at many of the country's finest dining establishments, developing dishes in my own restaurants, and cooking in my own kitchen at home. To me, it all falls within my happy zone.

I wrote this book, quite simply, for people who love to cook. Cooking should be inclusionary, not exclusionary. We gather in the kitchen because it's comforting, and it harkens back to the happy feelings that a warm, aromatic kitchen instilled in us as kids. Cooking and everything that goes with it is deeply engrained stuff, a connection to our childhoods that endures for a lifetime. At my house, for example, every Sunday night we had roast beef, simple vegetables, potatoes, and, occasionally, Yorkshire pudding. In adulthood, some of my best memories are of discovering foods while travelling, or dishes that came together while cooking alongside friends in the industry. Food is a connection to our past, our friends, our family, our culture, and the region in which we live. And I want to emphasize that you do not have to live anywhere near the Okanagan to enjoy the recipes in this book—my message, and

my philosophy, is to reap the rewards of your own region. If you live in an area that grows the best citrus fruits or avocados, or has an incredible maker of buffalo mozzarella, then those foods should become the heroes of your cooking. Every recipe in this book allows room for the cook to exercise some creative licence, and embrace their own unique regional best. Like I say, it's about connection.

My own earliest memory of where this passion for cooking first ignited was when I was about seven or eight years old. My father took me to visit a friend of his, who owned a hotel in Port Coquitlam, where I grew up. It was the kind of old-style hotel with separate entrances to the pub for gents and ladies, and sawdust on the floor. We toured the Chinese restaurant kitchen and the smells and the massive stainless steel stoves, the walk-in cooler, the pots and pans, the cooks at their stations—the intensity and bustle of it—just blew me away. I remember a giant maple chopping block that had a big dip in the middle from years of use. Today, I have my own maple chopping block, and even though the thing is 20 years old I still haven't put a dent in it.

For me, it's all about connecting with the freshest, highest-quality food and creating an exceptional meal. There is nothing that gives me greater pleasure than seeing the reaction to true, honest cooking. Home cooks know this feeling, too.

THE OKANAGAN VALLEY

LIVING IN THE FERTILE Kelowna region with its intensely hot, semi-arid summers makes it easy. Sourcing amazing product is simply a matter of dropping by the local farm, a few minutes' drive away. Every summer, the region explodes with apricots, peaches, sweet cherries, pears, plums, nectarines, grapes, and apples. The Okanagan Valley, 200 km long and 20 km wide, is home to some of B.C.'s most historic farmland. Take a drive around Kelowna, or Peachland or Penticton, and you can still see heritage orchards and farmhouses with their little cellars dug into the hillside, where potatoes, onions, carrots, and rutabagas were once stored before refrigeration became the norm.

The region has thousands of farms and makes up more than one-quarter of B.C.'s farming, but because there aren't big tracts of arable land, the farms are mostly small, family-run operations. The average farm size according to the 2011 census is about 76 acres, which isn't very big when you consider the average farm in Canada is 10 times that size. That limitation might make it difficult to pump out products on a mass scale, but the small farmer's dedication to their craft makes the Okanagan a local restaurateur's paradise.

As I discovered when I moved to the region years ago, it boasts the highest number of organic farms in the province. I try to keep it as local as possible. But I'll go outside of the Okanagan if I'm in search of a particular product, such as seafood from the coast, or bison from the Rocky Mountain foothills, or lamb from the Peace River region. If I can drive there and back in a day, I consider it locally sourced. That means I include the Fraser Valley and the Kootenays as part of my regional table. Today I buy from more than 150 regional suppliers, and while I obviously can't name them all, it's safe to say they all deserve a good share of credit for landing me my spot in the B.C. Restaurant Hall of Fame, and every other accolade I've received while living in the Okanagan. When I travel, I wave the Okanagan flag because I'm intensely proud of the world-class cuisine and hospitality of the region. That talent has kick-started a culinary tourism industry and as a result, the Okanagan Chefs Association is one of the largest and most vibrant in the country. As a chef, I consider it to be one of the most exciting regions — the consummate "chef's playground" because of the bevy of produce and meats, artisanal products, and award-winning wines.

When Rod and his business partner Audrey moved to the Okanagan it marked the start of a new era in the Okanagan culinary scene. When people of this calibre and experience come here, it brings a critical mass that attracts more.

HOWARD SOON

head winemaker, Sandhill Wines

The Okanagan is British Columbia's wine region, containing more than 80 percent of the province's vineyards, and is consistently ranked as one of the top producers of the world's best wines. The climate, as well as varying soil conditions across the valley, make it ideal for growing grapes. We weren't always known for our fine wines, but in 1989, when the province implemented the Vintners Quality Alliance (VQA), the bar was raised considerably. One of the early pioneers who helped put us on the map is Howard Soon, of world-renowned Sandhill Wines. Howard was the first winemaker to be awarded with a gold medal at the Chardonnay du Monde in France. In 2009, he also became the first winemaker to receive all three top honours at the Wine Access Canadian Wine Awards: Best Red Wine of the Year, Best White Wine of the Year, and Winery of the Year. "With the VQA wine industry, we've been making incredibly good wines year after year in the Okanagan, and it made the culinary scene pay attention," says Howard, who has 36 years of B.C. wine-making experience. The establishment of the VQA, he says, "just made the business case even stronger for fine dining and local suppliers."

And that's why the Okanagan is a chef's paradise. What would life be without fine food and fine wine?

HOW I DEVELOPED MY APPROACH TO COOKING

I'VE ALWAYS BELIEVED IN fresh, simple ingredients, but I fully realized my approach to food when I was a young chef working in Toronto.

In those early years, I worked in a lot of great kitchens, under a lot of tough, demanding chefs, who have all shaped my cooking approach. I landed a plum job at what is still one of Canada's finest eating establishments, Toronto's Scaramouche. While working there I learned that quality is in the details, from the fresh ground pepper to the best salt to the best cuts of meat and the freshest produce. Every ingredient was premium grade, and every cook and apprentice was qualified for the job. There were no short cuts or halfway measures. Even though I was too young to completely appreciate it, I remember Chef Russell Cottam wouldn't settle for anything less than the best raspberries he could find. And when they'd arrive through the back door, he'd get excited. That made an impression upon me — I was starting to learn.

But because I always wanted to work for the very best hotel, I made the leap to the Four Seasons. For a young chef, the Four Seasons Hotels and Resorts was literally the top of the food chain, and I was determined to get there. Every week I'd visit the Four Seasons Toronto Inn on the Park kitchen and ask for a job. The executive chef, Jurgen Petrick, would tell me I already had a good job and to go away. But once I got my Red Seal certification (a government program that requires a high level of technical training and many hours of apprenticeship), he relented and gave me a job, and I thrived in that kitchen. I learned firsthand what great service means. It means you pay attention to every detail, whether it's straightening the tablecloths or making sure the lights are soft and the music isn't too loud.

During my tenure at the Four Seasons, I had the honour of catering private dinner parties at the home of hotel chain founder Isadore Sharp and his wife Rosalie. I remember pulling up in the hotel van in the middle of winter and realizing the benefits of a heated driveway. It was an intimidating experience, preparing such an intimate dining service, but I learned to work through the nerves, and I loved it. Looking back, I am shocked that they gave a junior chef like me such a huge responsibility, but I'm glad they did. Catering those dinner parties was one of the most profound experiences of my career.

As for the food, it was the 1980s, and fine dining was big on rich, heavy sauces. But there was a move underway toward a cleaner, lighter approach to food, using reduction sauces, emulsions, and vinaigrettes. The Toronto kitchen was setting the direction for the rest of the chain, and I was excited to be at the forefront of the movement.

Also, the European-style outdoor food market had become popular, and it was there we'd source the freshest food for the evening's menu. That idea of using only the best ingredients became the gold standard I'd live by as a restaurateur.

When I decided to return to the West Coast, I landed a job at the Four Seasons Vancouver, under a young executive chef named Mark Baker. He taught me to work even harder, and to think like a team player. That came easily for me, because in my youth I was an aspiring baseball player, and naturally cocky and competitive. He set the bar high, and if you got on his good side, you were golden. That particular team of young chefs turned out to be a super group, and they went on to become some of the most influential chefs in the industry.

Kerry Sear, who replaced Mark, was one of those chefs. Kerry opened my eyes to the art of food and to the transformational aspects of cooking. Whether it was the unusual way he plated the food, or his wacky combinations of flavours, he was always pushing the boundaries. Working alongside someone who broke the rules, who marched to his own drum, really set off the creative part of my brain.

He also had the genius to hire Bernard Casavant as executive sous chef, who'd become one of the most influential chefs in my career.

Casavant, who's now based in Kelowna as well, is often called "the Alice Waters of B.C." Bernard and I bonded over our intense love of food, and we would debate the perfect way to cook wild rice without the grains exploding, or to prepare an ice wine dried fruit terrine—suffice it to say, we've been close friends since. We share an intense pride in being Western Canadian chefs, and we actively promote and advocate Canadian cuisine. Later, when he hired me as his executive sous chef and we opened the Chateau Whistler (it was a Canadian Pacific hotel in those days, and the first new Chateau hotel for CP in 100 years), we worked hard, clocking 14- to 16-hour days, and putting our regional-food-first philosophy to the test.

Bernard and I were both small-town Canadian boys, and we bonded immediately. We were both proud of being Canadian in a climate that too often celebrated European-trained chefs. We were also confident in our cooking, and we shared a ridiculously organized work ethic. I loved working with Bernard, but I was young and driven, and I wanted a job as top dog. So I took the executive chef job in the kitchen at the Pacific Palisades Hotel in Vancouver, which was

owned by the Shangri-La hotel chain, one of the top hotel chains in the world. I remember going for an interview and seeing the rooftop garden, and being blown away. I'd worked in a small way with an on-site herb garden before, but former chef Anne Milne had taken it to another level. And I expanded the garden further, with an abundance of herbs, flowers, and vegetables. This was at a time when nobody in the industry would have thought to do something like grow a garden within reach. I worked with general manager Stephen Darling, who is by far and away the most detail-oriented person I've ever met. Stephen was one of those people in my career who taught me the value of doing it right—again, nothing by half measures. He checked the way the napkins were folded, looked for lint on the carpet. Although he was general manager, he was very involved in every aspect of the restaurant, which was new to me at the time. At most hotels, the managers concerned themselves with the hospitality side of the business. But Stephen knew every detail of every dish, every aspect of service, and every wine. Each day, we would bake cookies for the guests who were checking in, and Stephen would check them for proper size and texture. Those damn cookies were the death of me. But I also greatly

respected that level of commitment to the job, and what he demanded from each of us.

Around this time, I was given the opportunity to work for Shangri-La in Hong Kong, which I jumped at, because working in Asia was on my bucket list. I also spent some time travelling through Singapore and Malaysia. And then the Wickaninnish Inn came calling. I was offered the opportunity to run a luxury restaurant in a new, large resort hotel that would be located on the wild, windswept western side of Vancouver Island, in the remote town of Tofino, a surfer's paradise. My business partner, Audrey Surrao, had at the time worked with a man named Charles McDiarmid, who was embarking on a major plan to open this luxury destination, to be called the Wickaninnish Inn. We'd be getting in on the ground floor, and I'd be able to create my own vision of the perfect restaurant. It was too good an opportunity to pass up.

When Charles brought me in as chef de cuisine at the Pointe Restaurant at the now legendary Wickaninnish Inn, I had a hand in everything: from construction and staffing to décor, menus, and even deciding on the bathroom towels. No detail was too small for my vision. I take a lot of pride in bringing the Pointe to such a level that the Wick earned the Relais & Châteaux designation only one year later.

The Relais & Châteaux is a prestigious 60-year-old French association that recognizes the finest hotels and restaurants in the world. They sent a judge out to spend the day reviewing the rooms, the grounds, the town, and finally the Pointe Restaurant. The tension was huge. Everybody was at the top of his or her game. At the end of the meal, Charles, the owner, remembers finally asking the French judge what he thought. He couldn't take the suspense any longer. When the judge proclaimed the Wick worthy of the Relais & Châteaux designation, Charles nearly did a jig. The judge said dinner that night is what clinched the deal for him to welcome us into the wonderful family of the Relais & Châteaux. The organization places a special focus on place and culture, which is what I already strived for at the Pointe. I scouted Vancouver Island for the finest salmon, halibut, albacore tuna, black cod, whatever came fresh off the boats, as well as the best farm-raised lamb or duck or artisanal cheeses. The best of the region always inspired my menu.

My years at the Wick were amazing, but the fog that rolled in off the open ocean of the west coast each summer was killing me. My contract was up, and although I loved my job, I needed the sun and I seriously needed to recharge. Nobody could believe I would want to leave the Wick,

We always had the vision that we wanted to be as known as a dining destination as we were known for accommodation. We even marketed the Pointe Restaurant separately. People would call and say, "Oh, and you have rooms too?" Rod was a part of making that a reality.

CHARLES MCDIARMID
owner of the Wickaninnish Inn

which had become world renowned by that point, but I've always followed my instincts. Audrey and I spent a good year or more travelling to places like India and Italy, which also influenced my approach to cooking. I was impressed by the Italians' intense respect for ingredients, and the Indian way of layering flavours.

Once we decided to get settled again, I realized that the sunny Okanagan would be my ideal cooking playground. Ingo Grady, director of wine education at Mission Hill Family Estate, played a big part in that decision. I'd known him for years, and I trusted his advice when he said that the Okanagan Valley was perfectly poised for a fine-

dining establishment run by a forward-thinking chef who was unabashedly proud of his West Coast roots.

When we relocated to Kelowna and launched Fresco in 2001, we hit the ground running with our fine-dining concept. Fresco was an instant hit — we earned the AAA Four Diamond Award in our first year, we won the Eat BC Restaurant of the Year award in 2008, and we were booked all the time. Ingo was right. We'd become a success story.

Although the economy took a hit of its own by 2008, it turned out to be our best year. But I predicted the mood for fine dining would start

to wane, and I knew it was time for a change. The economic downturn would surely have an impact in Canada. My instincts have always served me well, which has meant people are often shocked when I make a move that looks, from the outside, like it's coming out of left field. Audrey and I had already talked about opening a casual-dining establishment. When the downturn happened, we thought the time was ripe. We shut down Fresco, and re-opened in March 2009, at the same location, as RauDZ Regional Table. We were one of the first to make the switch in a long line of fine-dining restaurants that would do so.

We traded in the fuss of tablecloths for a decidedly food-centric approach. Drinks master Gerry Jobe started a revolution with his incredibly inventive and pioneering farm-to-table drinks menu. A 125-year-old reclaimed pine wood communal dining table, created by local craftsman Will Brundula, became the focal point of the room. The wine list was unabashedly dedicated to B.C. wines, and we tossed away the reservation book. On the walls were photographs of some of our suppliers. We operated by the motto: "Support local, buy local, eat and drink local." Pretty quickly, RauDZ was a success.

It's true cooking.
There are no smoke
and mirrors. You eat
that food, and you
know it came out
of his kitchen.

CHEF BERNARD CASAVANT
member of the B.C. Restaurant Hall of Fame

Four years later we opened a neighbouring cousin in order to handle the long line-ups of customers, and micro bar • bites has become a draw all of its own. I'm super proud of the design, by architect Tim Bullinger of Arca3 Design Studio. The room is a symphony of wood, with a custom-built, reclaimed wood U-shaped bar that pulls people together. The rows of vintage Edison lights that hang from the high ceiling create this warm, inviting atmosphere. Viewed through the big windows at night, it looks like a place that's buzzing with energy. Having a different concept from RauDZ, micro offers creative cocktails, international craft beers, Old World wines, and small, Mediterranean-inspired tapas plates, but the philosophy and the approach remain the same: quality, regional ingredients that add up to delicious.

In the spring of 2017, we added Terrafina at Hester Creek to the RauDZ Creative Concepts family. Chef de Cuisine Jenna Pillon also came on board, which means we have a culinary dream team. As for the location, it's ideal. The 95-acre Hester Creek Estate is located in Oliver, B.C., surrounded by hilly vineyards that are some of the oldest in the valley. The south Okanagan has far more in common with the Tuscany region of central Italy than it does with the famously rugged geography of B.C.'s west coast. It's a semi-arid climate, which is perfect for growing grapes, hence the area's nickname, "the Golden Mile." The Mediterranean-style views also provide the most beautiful backdrop for presenting our Italian riff on local ingredients, especially when dining on the patio, al fresco. Terrafina—Italian for "from the earth"—is my ode to the region, to the food, to the wine, and to the farmers and artisans of the south Okanagan.

Now that I'm pretty much a veteran in this industry, I'm also spending more time passing on my expertise to other young chefs, both at the restaurant and as an active member of professional chefs' organizations. I'm actively involved with the Canadian Culinary Federation and the Okanagan Chefs Association, but one of the initiatives dearest to my heart is the Okanagan Chefs Association's Chefs in the Classroom—Edible Education program, which teaches third-grade kids the value of locally grown food. The seven-lesson program culminates with a field trip to a working farm where we chefs prepare a big lunch for the kids. It's like regional food immersion 101, and for me it's a blast to see the kids realizing firsthand where their food comes from.

With experience comes a sense of responsibility, so I'm playing a bigger role in the community these days, too. We're a medium-sized business, but a lot of our corporate culture is about giving back—helping raise funds for better health care, the food bank, and community volunteer projects. We also try to minimize our carbon footprint. I own four bikes, and I'm happiest if I can pedal around town instead of driving. We support local suppliers, and try to hire talented local people before searching elsewhere. The way I see it, it's all fine and dandy to talk about sourcing local ingredients and being a regional establishment, but that philosophy has to extend to every aspect of life and business. Like Bernard says, "It's about connection."

THE FARM-TO-TABLE MOVEMENT

FARM-TO-TABLE is a movement in food that goes back to the 1970s, when chefs like California's Alice Waters began advocating for farm-fresh organic food, as opposed to packaged, processed, chemically sprayed, or genetically modified food. Before science started tampering with food, generations of people were eating organically without a second thought. Up until the era of frozen pizzas and Kool-Aid, people were getting by on canning and preserving and cellars full of root vegetables for the winter months. People like Waters, and environmentalist Wendell Berry and food writer Michael Pollan, raised alarm bells on how much we'd lost touch with the true value of food, both in terms of taste and nutrition.

Although I'm considered one of Canada's pioneers in the farm-to-table food movement, it's really just the way I evolved as a chef. I had already been sourcing the highest-quality ingredients on a mass scale at the hotels where I worked, so continuing the practice at my own restaurant was a given. People talk about organic food as if it's a specialty item — an exception, when it should be the rule. That's why you'll never see the word "organic" anywhere in my restaurants. Any chef worth his or her salt expects to cook with quality ingredients because they are the fundamentals of cooking.

Along its 120 kilometres of shore, Lake Okanagan offers up farms, vineyards, and passionate people intent on giving us the best of food and wine to share and enjoy. Our farm-to-glass cocktails, local brews, and wines that speak softly of their sense of place are the cornerstones of our local philosophy.

AUDREY SURRAO
of RauDZ Regional Table   micro bar · bites
Terrafina at Hester Creek by RauDZ

He was one of the first ones to really start buying local, especially organic. I guess in some of the other areas where he was chef, he was aware that organic produce tasted better than the chemical stuff. I don't know how many times I'd go in and congratulate him on an award, and he'd say to me, "It's your produce. I wouldn't win anything if your stuff didn't taste so good."

JON ALCOCK
owner of Sunshine Farm, one of the first organic farms in Kelowna

That means the fresher, the better. And that also means as little time spent in the back of a semi-trailer refrigeration unit as possible, which means that, ideally, the food is produced somewhere close to home. The wonderful thing about sourcing your food close to home is that you get to see where it's coming from. If you spend your weekends at farmers' markets, for example, you eventually get to know the farmers. You see who produces the finest heirloom tomatoes, peppers, and winter squash, and who invests their time producing unique varieties, like Kelowna's Purple Softneck garlic.

At RauDZ Regional Table, we have local farmers come in and give workshops in the kitchen on how to cook with 15 different varieties of radishes, or multicoloured heritage tomatoes, or uncommon herbs, such as winter thyme, summer thyme, Greek sage, variegated sage, and lime basil. The team and I also go out to the farms regularly, observing how food is grown and meat is butchered. Throughout the summer, we're canning and preserving fruits and vegetables to get us through the long winter months. We've got the process down so well, we sell RJB Blackberry Ketchup (and other preserves) as retail items. At the bar, our liquid chefs mix up drinks with regional tomatoes, smoked peppers, stone and tree fruits, and herbs.

We couldn't do any of this at our restaurants if we didn't have an up-close appreciation of the food. It is part of the job. A good cook spends as much time sourcing good-quality food as they do cooking. One of my suppliers, Sunshine Farm's Jon Alcock, grew up in the Okanagan, and he and his neighbours subsisted on the family garden. He remembers when a big grocery store moved to town and suddenly everybody was able to purchase Californian asparagus in December. But is it natural to be eating summer produce shipped in from afar in the dead of winter? Maybe we should be focusing on those starchy root vegetables instead. They're far fresher, higher in nutrients, and better for the environment, because they're locally sourced. I'm not saying everybody needs to start a massive garden and become self-sufficient, but I am saying that if we support local, we're going to personally benefit, and so will the communities we live in. It's a win-win.

HOW TO USE THIS BOOK

I WANT YOU TO get this book dirty—dog ear the pages, write in the margins, stuff your grandmother's best recipes for Swedish meatballs and zucchini loaf between these pages. Although if you'd like to reverently display it on a bookshelf or coffee table, I won't blame you. David McIlvride's photography is amazing. But I'd be more honoured if it spent the bulk of its time doing hard duty in your kitchen.

This book is structured in the order in which we enjoy our meals: sunrise, midday, sunset, and twilight. I'm a Leo who lives and cooks in the sunny Okanagan, so my life is already structured around the sun rising and setting, against the orchards, lakes, and hills of the valley. I give you recipes that take you from that first boost of the day to that well-deserved cocktail on a Friday night.

I've chosen the recipes in this book because they involve a skill set that ranges from super simple sandwich assembly to a serious amount of professional chef focus that will make the dish sing. Some recipes can be made in a pinch, which is basically how they were created. I opened the fridge without any master plan going in, and threw together something that would eventually become a go-to dish. That was the sort of improvisation behind my **Sharp Cheddar Scramble on PB Toast** [page 52]. On the other hand, there will be recipes that challenge you, too, and earn you cheers from all around the table. Those dishes, such as **Hot Smoked Salmon Fillets** [page 101] or **Venison Carpaccio** [page 80], require some technique and attention to detail.

I believe that there are essential elements that make food great. That require an understanding of the basics and a little ingenuity. This book is a distillation of my years of cooking experience. For a chef, creation is as much about the experiments that have gone wrong as it is about the magical moment when the heavens open and a dish totally comes together. It's a process of trial and error. Sometimes, it's a mistake that turns out to be brilliant.

Of course, the recipes embody my regional philosophy, which is to utilize those products closest to home. The recipes are simple and yet frequently decadent—and like most good things in life, they appear complex but are unabashedly straightforward. Whether it's my **Arctic char pressed in steel-cut or rolled oats** [page 154] or my **Bacon-Wrapped Plums with blue cheese mousse and port wine syrup** [page 221], the results will be amazing if you follow a few simple rules.

Before embarking on any recipe, it's essential that you have the proper equipment and ingredients beforehand. I'm including here a list of basic kitchen equipment that you'll need for the recipes. I've also listed basic pantry items that every home cook should have on hand. But there will be ingredients that you'll have to shop for, which is why you need to read through the recipe before getting started.

A big part of cooking is organization, and professional chefs know this, because it's part of the job. If we didn't stay organized, the service would fall apart pretty quickly, which would spell disaster for a restaurant. In my restaurant, the food delivered is inspected for freshness and quality when it arrives, the floors and ovens are cleaned every night, every utensil is in its place, every chef is at their station. Organization is essential to great cooking, and this goes for the home cook as well.

The French have a great phrase: *mise en place*. As a culinary term, it means prepping for the cooking, with all the ingredients measured and ready to go. It means the oven or BBQ is preheating and space has been made in the freezer or refrigerator if the dish you're making will need to chill. It means you won't be running around looking for that missing whisk when the time comes to whip those egg whites. It means you won't be throwing a piece of meat onto a cold pan, but a sizzling hot one. Do not be afraid of heat—it is a cook's best friend. A smoking hot pan sears and caramelizes the meat, giving it depth of flavour and holding in the juices. If you were to throw it onto a cold pan and bring it up to temperature, you'd end up steaming the meat and losing all that goodness. This is just one example of where home cooks can go wrong in the kitchen, and it comes back to doing your prep work. Oh, and always use fresh herbs instead of dried. They are infinitely superior.

I also want to emphasize that it's okay to substitute or omit ingredients when it makes sense. If the recipe calls for leeks and there are amazing cipollini onions at the market, for example, go right ahead and make the switch. If you despise cinnamon, simply omit it from the recipe. I personally don't love nutmeg and rarely cook with it. Obviously, the flavour profile should stay true to the recipe, but cooking calls for a degree of creative licence, so don't fear improvising. Tweak away. Make notes. I won't be offended.

It will also make the experience of cooking a stress-free and pleasurable one, which is what it's all about. This is, ultimately, the reason we cook. When I visit my chef friends at their homes, I'll stroll into the kitchen, pour myself a glass of wine, and without a second thought start stirring the sauce or soup they've got going on the stove. Cooking brings people together, and for my closest friends and me, it's a sort of language that we share. When you cook with passion, you feed the soul. So, think like a pro and do your prep work, stay organized, and enjoy yourself. Let's get cooking.

THE
ESSENTIALS

ORGANIZATION IS PARAMOUNT to good cooking. With so many affordable kitchen gadgets and appliances out there, I recommend making a nominal investment into these kitchen must-haves, which will make all the difference to your plated food. And I always make sure that my pantry is stocked with quality ingredients.

For the Kitchen

8- to 10-inch chef's knife

Blender (I still use my 30-year-old Osterizer so it doesn't have to be fancy)

Cast-iron skillet

Citrus press/juicer

Coffee grinder (for grinding spices only)

Fine-mesh strainer

Food processor (yep, I still use my 28-year-old Cuisinart)

Heavy-bottomed casseroles and pans

Japanese mandoline (for making very thin slices)

Masking tape and a Sharpie (for labelling and dating everything)

Nonstick skillets, small and large

Parchment paper

Pepper mill

Potato ricer

Small utility knife

For the Bar

Boston shaker

Hawthorne strainer

Long cocktail stir spoon

Muddler

Small fine-mesh strainer

In the Pantry

Black peppercorns

Extra-virgin olive oil

Good-quality stocks (preferably homemade)

Grapeseed oil

Red wine vinegar

Sea salt, fine and coarse

Spices (whole when possible)

White wine vinegar

NOTE *Let's talk for a moment about salt. I have on hand about a half-dozen salts at a time. All your ingredients should be quality ones, and that goes for the salt, too. In order to not over-salt, be sure to finish with it instead of starting with it. Your dish may taste properly seasoned at the beginning, but after a couple of hours of braising or simmering, once some moisture has evaporated, you could be stuck with a too-salty result.*

And if the dish contains a salty component such as bacon or anchovy, you might not even need to salt. I use a lot of lemon in my dishes, and lemon often replaces the need for more salt. In fact, if you're on a sodium-restricted diet, go for a squeeze of lemon instead. I always advise my young chefs to taste and taste again while cooking, and you should too.

SUNRISE

More than any other meal, the definition of breakfast is a highly personal one. Some people eat the exact same thing every morning, day in, day out.

OTHERS START THE DAY depending on their mood. And then some go all out on weekends and turn breakfast into a marathon cooking session, and feast like there's no tomorrow.

I love breakfast. It truly is the most important meal of the day, even if it's just a great piece of toast to get me started. On weekdays, I'm more of a **smoothie** man [page 41], because it's the best opportunity of the day for me to get my fruit and veg—some seasonal berries, a banana, yogurt, and spinach, and I give it a whirl. Of course, good coffee goes without saying. And if I do have a more substantial meal, it always involves eggs. My absolute favourite breakfast egg dish is also one of my oddest creations, involving **toast, peanut butter, green onions, sharp Cheddar cheese, scrambled eggs, and bacon** [page 52]. I stumbled upon this unlikely mix one bleary-eyed morning when I was camping as a youth, and it became my hearty breakfast go-to.

I've included that recipe here, so you can judge for yourself.

I've also included some basic breakfast dishes that might sound simple, but they work so well you'll come back to them again and again. My **Dried Fruit Granola** [page 45], for example, has been with me since I developed it back in my Four Seasons days in Vancouver. Of course, now I am living in orchard paradise, so I use Okanagan dried fruits. I use local fruits for other morning dishes as well, whether it's my tried-and-tested, fluffy, **world-famous pancakes** [page 48], **French Toast** [page 61], **Blackberry Yogurt and Hempseed Crunch** [page 42], or **Stewed Pears and Plums** [page 44]. And then there's my RJB **Blackberry Ketchup** [page 67], which is a bestseller at the restaurant, and marries beautifully with the **Cast-Iron Hash** [page 67]. I love pairing sweet and savoury, and you'll see that in a few dishes throughout this book.

And then there are the more decadent breakfast or brunch options, for those weekends when you want to indulge friends and family. On those occasions, serve **Potted Smoked Salmon and Bagel Crisps** [page 58] alongside **Poached Duck Eggs** [page 62], which I discovered in Italy, but made even more decadent with fresh shavings of Alba truffles. **The Potato Apple "Cake"** with rosti-style potatoes, eggs, and ham [page 51] also falls into that special occasion brunch category, and the ham can be swapped out for smoked salmon or trout, to elevate it even further.

The following recipes are some of my favourites, whether I'm looking for a simple but delicious burst of fuel, or a more sumptuous late-morning feast.

Everyday Smoothie

True to the name, I have this smoothie pretty much every single day, because
it's a great way to get my fruit and veggies without having to think about
it too much. (And first thing in the morning, I'm not ready to think too much.)
You can use any type of fruit that's in season, or swap out kale for spinach.
This particular combination is a tasty one that will recharge the batteries
and get you out the door.

INGREDIENTS

1 small banana

**6 fresh or frozen strawberries,
no need to thaw if frozen**

**⅓ cup fresh or frozen blueberries,
no need to thaw if frozen**

⅓ cup plain yogurt

¼ cup fresh-squeezed orange juice

12 spinach leaves

1 tsp vegetable powder

¾ cup chilled water

NOTE Vegetable powder can be found in
most large supermarkets or health food
stores. I use Genuine Health Greens +.

Serves 1 to 2

FIRST Combine all the ingredients in a blender, cover,
and blend on low speed. Gradually increase to high speed
and blend until smooth.

TO SERVE Pour into 1 or 2 glasses and serve immediately.

Blackberry Yogurt and Hempseed Crunch

This recipe is healthy, delicious, and easy peasy. Muddle your fresh fruit, mix with the yogurt, and toss on some crunchy hempseed. It's as simple as that. You can find hempseed at most health stores and it is rich in healthy fats, protein, and minerals. I always toast seeds, nuts, and spices because it gives a big boost of flavour. The toasted hempseeds will add nuttiness, and the mint and lemon will brighten up the whole dish.

INGREDIENTS

1 cup fresh blackberries, plus extra for garnish

1 cup vanilla or plain yogurt

⅓ cup toasted hempseeds

Finely grated zest of ¼ lemon

2 Tbsp chopped mint

Serves 2

FIRST Put the blackberries in a bowl and lightly mash. Add the yogurt and mix well, then divide the yogurt into 2 large glasses or bowls. Place in the fridge for 15 minutes to chill.

In a small bowl, combine the hempseeds and lemon zest and mix well.

TO SERVE Top each glass or bowl with the hempseed mixture, garnish with blackberries, and sprinkle the chopped mint on top. Serve immediately.

Stewed Pears and Plums

Fresh seasonal fruits stewed in warm spices have all the makings of ultimate comfort food. This recipe gets the most out of stone fruits from one season to the next, and I have several jars of these stewed pears and plums on hand at all times. They work as a cereal topping, or served with yogurt, cake, or ice cream.

INGREDIENTS

2 large pears, such as Red Bartlett, peeled, cored, and cut into wedges

2 cups fresh Italian prune plums, pitted, or 1½ cups prunes

1 cup apple juice

¼ cup granulated sugar

12 black peppercorns

5 cloves

2 cinnamon sticks

3 (2-inch) pieces orange zest

1 slice ginger

Hot cereal or granola, to serve

NOTE The syrup can be strained and spooned over cereal, ice cream, yogurt, or My World-Famous Pancakes (page 48).

Makes about 4 cups

FIRST Combine all ingredients in a pot. Bring to a simmer on medium heat, and cook for 20 minutes, or until fruit is tender. Chill. (The stewed fruit can be refrigerated, covered, for up to 2 weeks.)

TO SERVE Transfer to individual bowls and serve with your favourite hot cereal or granola.

Dried Fruit Granola

I developed this delicious healthy blend of dried fruit granola back in my days working at the Four Seasons in Vancouver. I've passed it on to other chefs I've worked with, and I continue to make it to this day. Now that I'm living in the Okanagan, I have a pretty amazing choice of fruits. And with the addition of so many dried fruits, this granola requires a lot less of the sugary syrup that is traditionally used. I've also added nutritious oat bran and quinoa for extra crunch, and cut way back on the usual amount of oil. You won't miss it.

INGREDIENTS

1 cup large-flake oats

½ cup oat bran flakes

¼ cup quinoa

¼ cup sunflower seeds

3 Tbsp sliced almonds

2 Tbsp grapeseed oil

½ Tbsp ground cinnamon

Pinch of salt

3 Tbsp honey

Finely grated zest of ½ orange

2 cups chopped dried fruit, such as peaches, pears, raisins, cherries, blueberries, figs, apricots, or apples

Milk or yogurt, to serve

Makes about 4 to 5 cups

FIRST Preheat oven to 375°F. Line a baking sheet with parchment paper.

In a large bowl, combine the oats, oat bran, quinoa, sunflower seeds, almonds, oil, cinnamon, and salt and mix well.

Spread the mixture evenly onto the prepared baking sheet and bake for 12 minutes, or until slightly brown. Transfer the mixture to a bowl, add the honey and orange zest, and mix thoroughly. Set aside to cool. Add the chopped dried fruit. (The granola can be stored in a zip-top bag or container for up to 1 month.)

TO SERVE Pour granola into a bowl and serve with milk or yogurt.

My World-Famous Pancakes

I've been making these pancakes since I was seven years old, and everyone loves them. The secret? Yogurt. I like vanilla yogurt, but you can use another flavour, or even plain. They magically puff up and take on a slight sourdough flavour. They are, quite simply, the best pancakes.

1 cup all-purpose flour

1 tsp baking powder

½ tsp baking soda

Pinch of salt

2 large eggs

¾ cup vanilla or fruit-flavoured yogurt

½ cup whole milk

1 tsp vanilla extract

Unsalted butter or grapeseed oil, for frying

1½ cups chopped seasonal fruit or berries (see Note), plus extra to serve

Your favourite syrup, to serve

NOTE Do not mix the fruit into the batter. Not only will it discolour the pancakes, it will cause uneven fruit distribution.

Makes 8 to 12 pancakes

FIRST In a medium bowl, sift the dry ingredients together.

In a separate bowl, combine the eggs, yogurt, milk, and vanilla and mix well.

Mix the wet ingredients into the dry ingredients, leaving it a bit lumpy.

Using a griddle or large nonstick pan over medium heat, heat 1 tablespoon of butter or oil. Ladle the batter into the pan to whatever size desired. Scatter 2 tablespoons of fruit over the pancake and cook for 4 to 6 minutes, until the bottom is golden. Flip and cook for another 3 to 4 minutes, until cooked through. Transfer to a plate and keep warm in the oven at 175°F. Repeat with the remaining pancakes.

TO SERVE Serve the pancakes with more fruit and your favourite syrup.

Potato Apple "Cake"

This dish is inspired by my travels through Germany and Switzerland.
I get the perfect texture by cooking my potatoes before I grate them.
You can serve the potato apple cake with a poached or fried egg and
high-quality ham. Smoked trout would go nicely, too.

INGREDIENTS

2 medium russet potatoes

1 small white onion, thinly sliced

2 small crisp apples, such as Braeburn,
peeled and coarsely grated (lightly
squeeze out excess moisture)

2 Tbsp chopped parsley, plus extra
for garnish

¼ tsp ground nutmeg

Salt and pepper to taste

3 Tbsp butter, pork fat, or duck fat

4 eggs, cooked to your choice

3 oz ham or smoked trout, thinly sliced

½ cup sour cream, to serve

¼ cup hot mustard, to serve

Serves 4

FIRST Preheat oven to 375°F and bake potatoes for 45 minutes,
until cooked through. Set aside to cool, then remove skin and
coarsely grate into a medium bowl. Add the onions, apples,
parsley, nutmeg, salt, and pepper, and mix until combined.

Heat a 10-inch cast-iron skillet or nonstick pan over medium
heat and add the butter (or fat). Put the potato mixture in the pan
and press down. Reduce the heat to medium-low and cook for
10 to 12 minutes, until the bottom is golden. (The heat is reduced
so the mixture will cook evenly.)

Using 2 frying spatulas, carefully flip the cake over and cook for
another 8 to 10 minutes, until golden. Transfer the cake to a large
serving plate and cut into 4 pieces.

TO SERVE Top each piece of the cake with an egg and a mound
of ham (or trout slices). Garnish with parsley and serve with the
sour cream and mustard.

Sharp Cheddar Scramble on PB Toast

This oddball dish is another one of my "what do I have in the fridge?" creations, but it also happens to be one of my absolute favourites. I could eat it any time of day. Extra-sharp Cheddar will hold its own alongside the soft scrambled eggs, the smoky bacon, the tangy green onions, and the naturally sweet peanut butter.

INGREDIENTS

4 slices double-smoked bacon, chopped

4 green onions, chopped

1 cup shredded sharp Cheddar

4 large eggs, beaten

2 to 3 Tbsp peanut butter

2 slices bread, toasted

Coarsely ground black pepper

Serves 2

FIRST Heat a nonstick skillet over medium-high heat, add the bacon, and cook for 3 to 5 minutes, until crispy. Add the green onions and cook for a minute. Add the Cheddar and eggs and cook for 2 to 4 minutes, until softly scrambled. Generously spread the peanut butter on both slices of toast.

TO SERVE Place a slice of peanut-buttered toast on each plate. Put the egg scramble on top and sprinkle with pepper.

Peach, Basil, and Sour Cream Muffins

I always make the most of each season's bounty, and these muffins are great at the height of summer, when fresh stone fruits and herbs are plentiful and at their best. Peach and basil are great partners. And the sour cream gives this muffin a moist texture that contrasts well with the crunchy oat topping. To further celebrate the fabulous fresh peaches, each muffin is topped with an extra wedge of peach and a dollop of sour cream.

INGREDIENTS

- ¼ cup (½ stick) unsalted butter
- ¾ cup brown sugar
- ¼ cup honey
- 2 eggs
- ½ tsp vanilla extract
- 2 cups all-purpose flour
- 1 tsp baking soda
- 1 tsp baking powder
- ½ tsp salt
- ½ cup whole milk
- ½ cup sour cream (divided)
- 3 peaches (divided)
- 8 basil leaves, chopped

CRUMBLE TOPPING

- 3 Tbsp oats
- 1 Tbsp all-purpose flour
- 1 Tbsp brown sugar
- 1 Tbsp unsalted butter, room temperature

Makes 12

FIRST Preheat oven to 325°F. Grease a 12-cup muffin pan or line with paper liners.

Using a stand mixer, cream together the butter, sugar, and honey. Add the eggs, one at a time, scraping down the sides of the bowl to ensure everything is mixed evenly. Stir in the vanilla.

In a large bowl, sift together the flour, baking soda, baking powder, and salt. Set aside.

In a small bowl, combine the milk and ¼ cup sour cream. Mix well, then add to the butter mixture.

Mix the wet ingredients into the dry ingredients until just combined. (Do not overmix.) Peel and pit 2 peaches and cut them into ½-inch cubes. Gently fold the chopped peaches and the basil into the batter. *Continued overleaf*

Spoon the batter into the muffin pan, filling the cups three-quarters full. Using a teaspoon, make a small well on the top of each muffin and spoon in 1 teaspoon of sour cream into each well. Peel and pit the remaining peach and cut it into 12 wedges, and put a slice on each muffin. (They don't need to be pressed into the batter.)

In a small bowl, combine the crumble topping ingredients, mix well, and generously sprinkle over the muffins. Bake for 30 minutes, or until a skewer or toothpick inserted into the centre of a muffin comes out clean.

TO SERVE When cool enough to handle, remove the muffins from the pan and set aside to rest for at least 10 minutes. Serve warm.

Potted Smoked Salmon and Bagel Crisps

This is my take on a classic breakfast bagel with cream cheese and lox.
You can buy good-quality smoked salmon if you're short on time, but this is a
good opportunity to smoke your own. It can be served in little Mason jars or
crocks as an appetizer, piped onto grilled baguette, or spread on cucumber
slices as canapés.

INGREDIENTS

2 shallots, finely chopped

1 stalk celery, finely chopped

½ cup white wine

1 cup (8 oz) cream cheese, room temperature

2 Tbsp chopped parsley

1 Tbsp chopped tarragon

Juice of ½ lemon

¼ tsp coarsely ground black pepper

3 oz sliced smoked salmon

2 Tbsp half-and-half (10%) cream

2 Tbsp roughly chopped celery leaves

2 unsliced bagels

Extra-virgin olive oil, for drizzling

Serves 2

FIRST In a small pot over medium-low heat, combine the shallots, celery, and white wine and cook for 4 to 6 minutes, until the wine has reduced by two-thirds. Set aside to cool.

In a food processor, combine the cream cheese, parsley, tarragon, lemon juice, black pepper, salmon, and cream and mix until completely smooth. Using a rubber spatula, scrape down the sides to ensure everything is mixed evenly. Transfer the mixture to a bowl, fold in the shallot and celery mixture, and add the celery leaves. Divide the smoked salmon mixture into 2 small crocks or Mason jars. Chill.

Preheat oven to 350°F. Thinly slice the bagels into disks and place on a parchment-lined or nonstick baking sheet. Drizzle with olive oil and bake for 10 minutes, until golden and crispy. (Keep an eye not to over-bake.)

TO SERVE Serve the potted smoked salmon with the bagel crisps.

French Toast

A plate of perfect French toast, served with fresh berries and syrup, is quintessential brunch fare. Thick slices of bread need to be properly soaked—as in, completely saturated in egg batter—by the time you get them to the pan. Also, don't be health conscious with this one: good-quality white bread absorbs the mixture best, and granulated sugar will caramelize so you get a brulée effect.

INGREDIENTS

3 large eggs

1¼ cups whole milk

¼ cup granulated sugar

1 Tbsp grated ginger

1 tsp ground cinnamon

¼ tsp coarsely ground black pepper

2 Tbsp dark rum (optional)

8 slices thick-cut potato bread or French bread

Butter or grapeseed oil

1½ to 2 cups raspberries or any seasonal berries

Maple syrup, to serve

Serves 4

FIRST In a large bowl, combine the eggs, milk, sugar, ginger, cinnamon, pepper, and rum, if using. Whisk together until well mixed.

Preheat a griddle or large nonstick pan over medium heat. Fully soak a slice of bread in the egg mixture, turning to immerse both sides. Add the butter or oil to the pan, place the battered bread into the pan, and cook for 5 to 7 minutes, until golden brown. Flip and cook for another 3 to 4 minutes, until golden brown. Keep warm in the oven at 175°F. Repeat with the remaining bread.

TO SERVE Serve the French toast on a platter or divide the pieces evenly between 4 plates. Top with berries and lots of maple syrup. The diet starts tomorrow!

Poached Duck Eggs

I stumbled upon this dish while taking a salumi course in Italy with three other chef friends. We rented a flat in Alba for the truffle festival, and one morning we had the most indulgent breakfast: poached eggs served with shaved Alba truffles and a drizzle of high-quality extra-virgin olive oil. Most people are unlikely to have truffles handy, so I haven't included them in the recipe, but it won't matter. The specialness of the duck eggs alone takes this dish to another level.

INGREDIENTS

6 cups water

Splash of distilled white vinegar

4 duck eggs

4 thick slices baguette

4 to 6 Tbsp extra-virgin olive oil

3 Tbsp chopped flat-leaf parsley

1 Tbsp lovage or celery leaves

2 tomatoes, chopped, or ¾ cup halved cherry tomatoes

Coarse sea salt

Coarsely ground black pepper

Serves 2

FIRST Pour the water into a shallow pot and bring to a boil over high heat. Add the vinegar, reduce to medium-low heat, and gently simmer. Crack the eggs into 4 separate small bowls. Carefully add each egg into the simmering water and cook for 6 minutes, for a soft-medium doneness.

TO SERVE Put 2 slices of baguette onto each of 2 plates. Using a slotted spoon, transfer the duck eggs onto each slice. Generously drizzle the olive oil over the eggs and top with parsley, lovage (or celery leaves), and chopped tomatoes. Season with salt and pepper. Serve immediately.

Frittata

Frittatas are incredibly versatile: I take stock of whatever is in my fridge that morning and use it as my guide. With my trusty and perfectly seasoned cast-iron pan, I know I can get an even temperature that will turn out the perfect frittata. (I even have a tiny cast-iron pan for a one-egg frittata.) If you're entertaining, I recommend pre-making these and reheating them for brunch. Your guests won't be disappointed.

INGREDIENTS

¼ cup olive oil (divided), plus extra for greasing

1 red onion, thinly sliced

Salt and black pepper

1 zucchini, sliced into thin rounds

3 chorizo or fresh Italian sausages, casings removed and diced small

⅓ cup sun-dried tomatoes, finely chopped

⅓ cup chopped basil

¼ cup chopped parsley

4 oz chèvre (fresh goat cheese), crumbled

1 (2-oz) bag plain potato chips, coarsely crushed

6 eggs, beaten

Favourite condiment, to serve

Serves 4 to 6

FIRST In a medium skillet over medium heat, heat 1 tablespoon oil, then add the onions and sauté for 3 to 5 minutes, until slightly cooked. Season with salt and pepper. Transfer to a bowl and set aside.

In the same skillet over medium heat, add another tablespoon of oil and the zucchini, and sauté for 3 to 4 minutes, until slightly cooked. Season with salt and pepper. Transfer to a bowl and set aside.

In the same skillet over medium heat, add 2 more tablespoons of oil and the chorizo (or Italian sausage), and cook for 3 to 5 minutes, until slightly brown. (If using fresh sausage, cook until cooked through.) Remove and set aside.

Preheat oven to 375°F. Use oil to grease a 12-inch round ovenproof pan (or use nonstick spray). Arrange the zucchini slices on the bottom, add the red onions, and spread out evenly. Scatter over the sausage, sun-dried tomatoes, basil, parsley, and chèvre. Sprinkle the potato chips on top, then slowly pour the beaten eggs into the entire pan, and lightly shake the pan to distribute the egg evenly. Bake for 35 to 45 minutes, until the egg has set and the frittata has pulled away from the edges. Set aside for 10 minutes, until cooled.

TO SERVE Turn the frittata onto a serving plate, cut into wedges, and serve.

✛ **Our famous Okanagan Fruit Sangria [page 239]**

Cast-Iron Hash

To make this hash dish sing, I'm sharing with you the recipe for *the* best-selling product from our restaurant: our RJB Blackberry Ketchup. While it may sound sweet, there are enough complex flavours in this recipe to keep it savoury, and it's a delicious substitute for regular tomato ketchup. The recipe here yields four cups, which can be canned for future use, so you can use it on a grilled cheese sandwich, leftover meatloaf, or French fries.

INGREDIENTS

¼ cup olive oil

3 yellow potatoes, skin on and cut into ½-inch cubes

3 shallots, sliced

5 green onions, chopped

1 cup shredded cooked chicken

⅔ cup cooked black beans

3 Tbsp chopped tarragon

Salt and black pepper

4 large eggs, cooked to your choice

2 tomatoes, cut into wedges

RJB BLACKBERRY KETCHUP

2 Tbsp olive oil

1 onion, chopped

8 cloves garlic, chopped

8 whole cloves

½ Tbsp dry mustard

1 tsp ground cinnamon

1 tsp ground allspice

1 tsp ground paprika

¼ tsp chili flakes

4 cups fresh blackberries (or 3 cups frozen)

1½ cups canned tomatoes

¼ cup brown sugar

¼ cup red wine vinegar

1 sprig rosemary, leaves chopped

1 tsp thyme leaves

Serves 4

RJB BLACKBERRY KETCHUP In a medium pot over medium heat, heat the oil, add the onions and garlic, and sauté for 2 to 3 minutes, until softened. Add the cloves, mustard, cinnamon, allspice, paprika, and chili flakes and cook for a minute, until fragrant. Add the remaining ingredients and bring to a simmer. Reduce to low heat, cover, and cook for another 45 minutes, stirring occasionally.

Transfer the mixture, in batches, to a blender and purée until completely smooth.

Strain through a fine-mesh strainer. Stir, transfer to a bowl or sterilized jar, and chill. Makes 4 cups. (It can be refrigerated for up to 1 month or use canning process in jars to keep longer.)

NEXT To make the hash, heat a cast-iron skillet over medium-high heat. Add the oil and potatoes and sauté for 25 minutes, until tender. Add the shallots and cook for another 2 minutes. Add the green onions, chicken, black beans, and tarragon and cook for another 4 to 6 minutes, until warmed through. Season to taste with salt and pepper.

TO SERVE Transfer the hash to 4 individual plates, top with eggs, and serve blackberry ketchup and fresh tomato wedges on the side.

Sunday Sandwich

I love sandwiches and I love breakfast, so voilà: the Sunday Sandwich. The recipe features a blend of Indian-inspired spices, plus there's crunchy almonds and rich pork belly, balanced out with the sharp acidity of the green tomato chutney. I often tell my staff that every ingredient in a recipe must serve a purpose, and this dish illustrates that perfectly in its layering of flavours. As the sandwich requires some time to prepare, I recommend planning ahead and cooking the pork in advance.

INGREDIENTS

1 lb pork belly
1 Tbsp coarsely ground black pepper
1 tsp ground smoked paprika
¼ tsp salt
½ cup water
4 large eggs
1 cup green tomato chutney
8 slices whole grain bread, toasted
1½ cups alfalfa sprouts

GREEN TOMATO CHUTNEY

2 Tbsp grapeseed oil
1 small onion, finely chopped
4 cloves garlic, crushed
1 Tbsp grated ginger
4 large green tomatoes
½ cup raisins
¼ cup apple juice
¼ cup brown sugar
2 Tbsp white wine vinegar
2 Tbsp slivered almonds
1 Tbsp pink peppercorns
1 tsp ground cardamom
1 tsp ground cumin
½ tsp ground turmeric
¼ tsp chili flakes
1 Tbsp chopped flat-leaf parsley
Finely grated zest of 1 orange
Salt and pepper

Serves 4

FIRST Preheat oven to 350°F. Put the pork belly in an oven-proof dish, rub with pepper, paprika, and salt, and add water. Cover with foil and cook for 1½ hours, or until tender. Remove and let cool.

GREEN TOMATO CHUTNEY In a medium pot over medium heat, combine the oil, onion, garlic, and ginger, and sauté for 2 to 3 minutes, until softened. Add the remaining ingredients, cover, and simmer for 30 to 45 minutes. Season with salt and pepper to taste. Set aside to cool. (Makes about 4 cups.)

TO ASSEMBLE Slice pork belly into 8 pieces. In a small skillet over medium heat, add the pork belly and gently fry for 3 to 5 minutes. Flip over and cook for another 2 to 3 minutes. Transfer to a plate and keep warm. (Leave the fat in the pan.)

In the same pan, fry the eggs over medium heat for 4 to 5 minutes, or until the yolks are almost cooked medium-well.

TO SERVE Spread the chutney on 4 pieces of toast, and top each with sprouts, 2 slices of pork belly, one egg, and the remaining toast.

✚ **Blue Mountain Vineyards   2012 Brut Rosé   Okanagan Falls**
Lovely pink colour, fresh strawberries on the nose, and crisp mousse

NOTE The leftover chutney can be refrigerated in a covered container for up to 2 weeks. To save yourself time, the chutney can also be made in large batches and canned.

MIDDAY

One of my
most satisfying
moments as a
chef was back
in 2001, when
we were still
running Fresco
Restaurant &
Lounge.

THE PHONE IN THE KITCHEN RANG and on the other end of a bad connection was a man from Sault Ste. Marie. He had visited the restaurant with his mother, and her dying wish was to have our **Spring Pea Soup** [page 86] one more time. What else could we do? We packed some soup into a Thermos and flew it to Sault Ste. Marie. Her grateful son called me a day later, quite overcome to see his mother's wish fulfilled. It was one of those defining moments where you realize what a huge impact your work can have on someone's life. Like I always say, food truly unites us, even a humble pea soup. That soup—made with fresh spring peas—is delicious, by the way.

So, I've included my Spring Pea Soup here, along with some other beloved recipes that go back over the decades I've worked as a chef. These are dishes best served at midday, when we crave a hot soup, or a hearty sandwich, or a light and refreshing salad. I've included some desserts too, because if you're like me, you'll want to balance out a good meal, even at midday, with a satisfying, sweet ending.

And, of course, there are the bestsellers from the restaurant that I simply have to include (or my regular customers won't forgive me). The **Chickpea-Battered Fish and Chips** [page 92] fall into this category. My version—influenced by my travels in India—is gluten free with chickpea flour batter. **Venison Carpaccio** [page 80] is another hit, served with some shaved apple and a little mustard dressing for acidity. It's a great opportunity to practise your knife skills, because carpaccio is all about slicing the meat ultra-thin, so it practically melts in your mouth. If you want a bit more of a challenge, the **Halibut Pastrami** [page 99] recipe is easy to follow, but it takes some extra time. And it's well worth it.

You'll see that with our **Crab Cakes** [page 96], we don't use any fillers—this is Dungeness crab, front and centre. Then there is my love of the sandwich. I grew up on sandwiches, and you'll always find a loaf of good-quality bread in my kitchen. And cheese. I am a man who loves his cheese. But if I were stranded on a desert island with one sandwich, I would choose the humble tomato sandwich—good bread, a little butter, mayonnaise or olive oil, sweet, just-picked tomatoes, and salt and pepper. To me, that's pure heaven. But you don't need a recipe to follow for that one.

Instead, I give you my take on the BLT, which goes coastal: the **Sockeye Salmon BLT** [page 107]. When I create a dish, it's all about balance, and in this one, the richness of the salmon is offset by the saltiness of the pancetta.

For a showy dish that will make a lasting impression on guests, there's the **Pear and Brie Flatbread** [page 75] with hazelnut pesto. Flatbread is deceptively easy to make, and everybody loves sharing bread. It's basically fancy pizza. As with a lot of my recipes, feel free to get creative and improvise.

And remember, we eat with our eyes. Finish a dish with a scattering of fresh herbs, for example. Maybe you prefer a thin slice of lemon or a drizzle of honey. Remember, the more beautiful it is, the faster your guests will want to dig in.

Pear and Brie Flatbread

Juicy pear and creamy, salty brie make for a classic flavour combo. The arugula gives an assertive pepperiness and the micro-grated hazelnut adds crunch. Don't have pear and brie? Try thinly sliced apple and Parma ham, or peach with chèvre.

FLATBREAD

1⅛ tsp active yeast

3 tsp granulated sugar (divided)

1 cup warm water

2¼ cups all-purpose flour

½ tsp salt

2 Tbsp olive oil

Cornmeal, for sprinkling (optional)

3 large pears, cored and cut into ¼-inch wedges

8 oz brie, sliced

2 generous handfuls arugula, for garnish

3 to 5 hazelnuts, finely grated, for garnish

Coarse sea salt and freshly ground black pepper

HAZELNUT PESTO

½ cup basil leaves

½ cup arugula

¼ cup grated Parmigiano-Reggiano

¼ cup extra-virgin olive oil

¼ cup hazelnuts

5 cloves garlic

NOTE The dough can be prepared in advance. After punching the dough, wrap it tightly in plastic wrap, and refrigerate for up to 1 week or freeze for up to 1 month.

Makes 2 (8- × 12-inch) flatbreads

FLATBREAD In a small bowl, combine the yeast, 1½ teaspoons sugar, and the water, stir, and set aside for 5 minutes to activate the yeast.

Meanwhile, in a large bowl, combine the flour, remaining 1½ teaspoons sugar, salt, and olive oil and mix well. Pour in yeast mixture, mix well, and knead for 5 to 8 minutes. (Alternatively, transfer the mixture to a mixer with a dough hook attachment and knead for 5 minutes.) This will be a wet dough. Cover with plastic wrap and set aside in a warm area of the kitchen for 30 to 45 minutes, until the dough has doubled in size. Punch down and divide the dough, then cover and refrigerate until use.

HAZELNUT PESTO Combine all the ingredients in a food processor and purée until smooth. (Makes ¾ cup.)

TO ASSEMBLE Preheat oven to 425°F. Line 2 medium baking sheets with parchment paper and sprinkle with cornmeal, if using.

Stretch and roll out one portion of the dough to an 8- × 12-inch rectangle. Repeat with the other half. Place the dough on the prepared baking sheets.

Spread the hazelnut pesto over the 2 pieces of dough, and then arrange the pear wedges on top to cover most of the surfaces. Bake for 10 minutes. Add the sliced brie and bake for another 4 to 8 minutes, or until the flatbreads are baked through.

TO SERVE Cut the flatbread into pieces, garnish with arugula and hazelnuts, and season with salt and pepper.

✚ **Gray Monk Estate Winery** | **2014 Pinot Gris** | **Lake Country**
Pear, apple, and white peaches with a hint of lemon citrus

Tomato and Watermelon Salad

Never underestimate the power of simplicity. The unlikely flavour combination of watermelon, tomato, and mint is fantastic, and I highly recommend you seek out camelina oil, which adds ample dimension to the flavour profile. The emphasis here is freshness, so you'll want the best tomatoes.

INGREDIENTS

2 lbs mixed heirloom tomatoes

2 cups watermelon cubes

¼ cup mint leaves

3 Tbsp camelina oil (see Note)

Sea salt and coarsely ground black pepper

NOTE Camelina oil is a light, nutty, and earthy oil that comes from the seeds of *Camelina sativa*, otherwise known as false flax. It can be found in specialty food stores. (Three Farmers in Saskatchewan is a good online source.)

Serves 4

FIRST Using a sharp knife, core the tomatoes and cut them into a variety of shapes, such as slices, wedges, or halves. Combine the tomatoes and watermelon cubes on a serving platter, scatter over the mint leaves, and drizzle with camelina oil. Season with salt and pepper.

TO SERVE Serve the salad on the platter, family style.

Summer Greek-Style Salad

With plump tomatoes, bell pepper, romaine, and chickpeas, this not-so-classic
Greek salad is packed with an abundance of summer produce. If you don't
have the time (or inclination) to soak dried chickpeas overnight, it's perfectly
acceptable to use canned chickpeas. However, be sure to use a good-quality
olive oil that smells as lively and vibrant as it tastes.

INGREDIENTS

½ **head romaine lettuce,
finely chopped and small centre
leaves set aside for garnish**

½ **cup crumbled feta cheese**

¾ **cup diced tomatoes**

1 **medium bell pepper (any colour),
seeded and diced**

¼ **cup pitted sun-dried olives**

½ **cup chickpeas, soaked overnight
(or canned chickpeas, rinsed)**

8 **basil leaves, roughly chopped**

1 **Tbsp oregano leaves**

12 **chives, cut into 1-inch lengths**

Juice of 1 lemon

3 **Tbsp good-quality extra-virgin
olive oil**

**Sea salt and coarsely ground
black pepper**

Serves 2 to 4

FIRST In a large bowl, combine all the ingredients and toss well
to mix. Season with salt and pepper.

TO SERVE Transfer to a serving bowl and garnish with the tiny
romaine leaves.

+ **Hester Creek Estate Winery** | **2015 Trebbiano** | **Oliver**
Light, bright, and crisp with lemony citrus

Venison Carpaccio

As venison is more readily available these days, this popular RauDZ menu item can be easily re-created at home. The greatest challenge is getting that paper-thin slice, so freezing the meat beforehand is essential. Then, it all comes together with the pepperiness of the watercress, the acid of the mustard dressing, and the sweetness of the apples.

INGREDIENTS

1 tsp coarsely ground black pepper

1 Tbsp thyme leaves

1 Tbsp chopped parsley

1 tsp chopped rosemary

1 (8- to 10-oz) boneless venison loin, tenderloin, or Denver leg (see Note)

1 Tbsp grapeseed oil

1 medium apple, cored and very thinly sliced, for garnish

Mustard Dressing (recipe here)

Watercress, for garnish

¼ cup toasted walnuts, for garnish

Coarse sea salt

1 to 2 baguettes, sliced and grilled (3 to 4 slices per person)

MUSTARD DRESSING

1 medium shallot, finely chopped

2 cloves garlic, finely chopped

2 Tbsp white wine vinegar

2 Tbsp grapeseed oil

1 Tbsp honey

1 Tbsp Dijon mustard

1 Tbsp finely chopped chives

NOTE A Denver leg is a cut that comes from the hind leg. Trimmed of the silver skin and fat, this cut is very versatile and ideal for roasts, stir-fries, steaks, and stews. Beef, veal, or bison may be substituted if venison is unavailable—the key is to buy a high-quality, sinew-free cut of meat.

Serves 4 to 6

CARPACCIO Rub the pepper, thyme, parsley, and rosemary onto the venison. Heat a cast-iron skillet over medium-high heat until hot. Add the venison, drizzle over the oil (careful of splatters), and brown for 4 to 6 minutes. Continue to turn and sear until you have a nice brown crust over the entire surface. Remove the venison from the pan and, when cool enough to handle, wrap tightly in plastic wrap. Wrap in a layer of foil to make it even tighter (to hold the shape). Put in the freezer and freeze for 4 to 6 hours, until completely frozen.

MUSTARD DRESSING In a small bowl, combine all the ingredients and mix well. Refrigerate until use.

TO ASSEMBLE Remove the venison from the freezer and set aside for 20 minutes so it's slightly defrosted but not completely thawed. (This will help you slice the meat easier.) Slice the venison as thin as possible, and, working quickly, arrange the slices on individual plates or a serving platter. (It's easier to handle the delicate slice while still slightly frozen. They thaw out quickly once they're sliced.)

Top with the sliced apples, allowing the carpaccio to show through. Drizzle with mustard dressing and generously garnish with watercress and walnuts.

TO SERVE Sprinkle the venison carpaccio with coarse sea salt and serve with the toasted baguette slices.

✛ **Haywire Winery** | **2014 Gamay Noir** | **Summerland**
Soft red with plush gentle tannin structure

Fresh Sablefish Niçoise

Sablefish is a west coast delicacy that tends to be on the fatty side, so you don't need big portions. I serve it as a take on a traditional French Niçoise salad, with green or yellow beans, tomatoes, boiled egg, and fresh oregano. Make the salad component ahead of time so you can concentrate on cooking the fish to perfection, because it is the star.

INGREDIENTS

2 new potatoes

¾ cup green and/or yellow beans, trimmed and cut into 2-inch pieces

¾ cup cherry tomatoes, halved

1 hard-boiled egg, thinly sliced

3 green onions, chopped

3 anchovies, finely chopped

2 Tbsp balsamic vinegar

3 Tbsp extra-virgin olive oil (divided)

1 Tbsp chopped parsley

1 Tbsp chopped oregano

Sea salt and coarsely ground black pepper

2 (5-oz) skinless sablefish fillets

1 Tbsp unsalted butter

Serves 2

FIRST Bring a pot of salted water to a boil, add the potatoes, and simmer for 15 to 20 minutes, until tender. Drain, set aside to cool, and then thinly slice.

Bring a separate pot of salted water to a boil, add the beans, and blanch for 30 to 45 seconds. Using a slotted spoon, transfer the beans to a bowl of ice water to stop the cooking. Drain.

Combine the potatoes, beans, tomatoes, egg, and green onions in a bowl and set aside.

In a small bowl, combine the anchovies, vinegar, 1 tablespoon olive oil, parsley, and oregano and whisk. Pour the dressing over the salad mixture and gently mix. Season with salt and pepper. Set aside.

In a medium skillet over medium-high heat, heat the remaining 2 tablespoons oil. Pat-dry the sablefish with a paper towel, then season with salt and pepper. Put the fish into the pan and cook for 3 minutes. Add butter, spoon the melted butter over the fish, and cook for another 2 minutes, until a nice crust has formed. Flip the fish over and cook for another 3 minutes, until the fish is just cooked through. (Do not overcook.)

TO SERVE Transfer the salad to 2 plates, top with the sablefish, and spoon any pan drippings over the fish. Serve immediately.

✛ **Blue Mountain Vineyards**   **2015 Sauvignon Blanc**   **Okanagan Falls**
Grassy, herbaceous notes, and crisp acidity

Braised Beets and Crumbled Chèvre

Whether slow-roasted in an oven to enhance their natural sweetness, puréed into a soup, or thinly sliced and served raw in a fresh salad, beets are incredibly versatile. I particularly enjoy them braised, when they take on the flavours of the aromatics, and their colour and flavour intensify.

INGREDIENTS

2 lbs small mixed beets, such as red, gold, and striped, skin on

6 oz chèvre (fresh goat cheese), crumbled

Sunflower sprouts, for garnish (optional)

Sea salt and coarsely ground black pepper

Any type of crackers

BRAISING

5 cloves garlic

1 medium onion

2 sprigs rosemary

1 bunch thyme

6 juniper berries

6 whole cloves

1 cinnamon stick

1 Tbsp coriander seed

1 tsp black peppercorns

1 tsp salt

3 cups water

½ cup raspberry vinegar (can be found at specialty grocery stores; I like the Vinegar Lady's)

Serves 4

FIRST Preheat oven to 375°F. Place beets in an ovenproof casserole dish, add the braising ingredients, and mix well. Cover with foil or a lid and braise in the oven for 1 ½ to 2 hours, or until beets are tender. Remove the dish from the oven and set aside to cool.

Peel the beets and discard the braising liquid. Cut the larger beets into wedges or slices and transfer to a large serving platter or 4 individual plates.

TO SERVE Top the beets with the crumbled chèvre, garnish with sunflower sprouts, if using, and season with salt and pepper. Serve with crackers on the side.

✛ Autumn in the Valley cocktail [page 222]

Spring Pea Soup

When the peas are just picked and bursting with flavour, this dish is a springtime favourite. The combination of pea with mint is classic, and our version of this soup is one of our bestsellers. This is an excellent soup to serve chilled.

INGREDIENTS

½ cup (1 stick) unsalted butter

1 medium onion, finely chopped

2 stalks celery, finely chopped

½ cup sliced leeks

6 button mushrooms, sliced

4 cloves garlic, finely chopped

3 bay leaves

½ tsp black peppercorns

4 sprigs mint

3 cups vegetable stock

1 cup whipping (35%) cream

3 cups peas, thawed if frozen

1 cup spinach leaves

Sea salt and black pepper

Serves 4 to 6

FIRST In a large pot over medium heat, melt the butter until it starts to bubble. Add the onions, celery, leeks, mushrooms, and garlic and sauté for 5 to 7 minutes, until the vegetables have softened. (Reduce heat if the vegetables start to colour.)

Add the bay leaves, peppercorns, mint, stock, and cream and mix well. Gently bring soup to a near boil, reduce the heat to medium-low, and simmer, partially covered, for 30 to 40 minutes. Stir occasionally.

Remove the soup from the heat and strain through a fine-mesh strainer into another pot or container. Discard the vegetables.

Put 1 cup of peas and a third of the spinach into a blender, pour in a third of the hot liquid, and blend on low heat. Gradually switch to a high speed and blend until very smooth. (Stop and allow some of the steam to escape while blending to avoid splattering.) Strain through a fine-mesh strainer into a saucepan. Repeat this process in thirds until all of the peas, spinach, and liquid are blended. Whisk the soup and season to taste with salt and pepper.

TO SERVE Heat the pea soup to serve, or refrigerate until use, if serving chilled.

✛ **Gehringer Brothers Estate Winery** | **2013 Classic Riesling** | **Oliver**
Stone fruits balanced with lively acidity

Heirloom Tomato and Blue Cheese Tart

Don't pussyfoot around this one. You want big flavours, with chunks of blue cheese, big pieces of basil, and slices of raw, sweet onion. As any kind of blue cheese can be used in this tart, I consider this your opportunity to make friends with your local cheese maker. This tart makes a fantastic dinner-party dish. Prepare it in advance and reheat just before serving, which will allow the filling to set properly.

INGREDIENTS

3 oz Terroir blue cheese or any mild blue cheese, cut into small chunks

¾ to 1 cup Custard Filling (recipe here)

Handful of arugula or mustard greens

½ medium sweet onion, such as Vidalia or Walla Walla

PASTRY

2 cups all-purpose flour, plus extra for dusting

1 cup (2 sticks) cold butter, cut into ¼-inch cubes

¼ tsp salt

1 egg

2 Tbsp ice-cold water

ROASTED TOMATOES

4 medium heirloom tomatoes, cut in wedges or halved

2 Tbsp olive oil

¼ cup basil leaves

Sea salt and coarsely ground black pepper

CUSTARD FILLING

2 eggs

½ cup milk

⅓ cup whipping (35%) cream

Sea salt and coarsely ground black pepper

Makes 1 (10-inch) tart

PASTRY Using a stand mixer, combine the flour, butter, and salt and mix on low speed, until it has a pea-like consistency. (Alternatively, use your hands by working the mixture quickly through your fingers and palms.)

In a small bowl, combine the egg and water together, mix well, and add to the flour mixture. Mix until the dough just comes together. (Do not overmix.)

Turn the dough out onto a floured surface and shape into a rectangle. Wrap the dough tightly with plastic wrap and refrigerate until use.

ROASTED TOMATOES Preheat oven broiler to high. In a medium bowl, combine the tomatoes, oil, and basil. Add salt and pepper to taste and toss to mix. Transfer the mixture to a roasting pan and place on middle shelf in oven. Broil for 5 to 8 minutes, until the tomatoes are slightly browned and slightly dried. Remove and set aside. *Continued overleaf*

CUSTARD FILLING Combine all the ingredients in a medium bowl and mix well. Set aside.

Preheat oven to 425°F. Roll the dough out to a circle, about 12 inches in diameter, and then press the dough into a 10-inch tart pan (preferably one with a removable base). Using the rolling pin, roll over the top edge of the pan to trim the dough. Refrigerate until ready to make the tart.

TO ASSEMBLE Arrange the tomatoes, face side up (if using halves), in the pastry-lined tart pan. Pour the custard filling around tomatoes, sprinkle with blue cheese, and cover loosely with foil. Bake on lower rack of the oven for 15 minutes, then reduce temperature to 375°F and bake for another 30 minutes, until the pastry is golden and cooked through. Remove from the oven and set aside to rest for 15 minutes.

TO SERVE Cut the tart into wedges and serve with fresh arugula (or mustard greens) and sliced onion rings on top.

RED 8.16
CABBAGE

Chickpea-Battered Fish and Chips

This Indian-inspired take on classic fish and chips is a favourite on the menu. Chickpea flour, also known as gram or garbanzo flour, is a staple in India and I use it here to achieve a crisp, nutty batter that can't be achieved with other flours. As I've noted previously, toasting certain ingredients brings out flavour, so be sure to toast the chickpea flour.

INGREDIENTS

3 cups canola oil, for deep-frying

1 lb snapper, cod, or halibut, cut lengthwise into 2-inch-wide strips

1 Tbsp chopped cilantro

Sea salt and coarsely ground black pepper

CHICKPEA BATTER

½ cup chickpea flour

¾ cup warm water

1 tsp chili powder

TARTAR SAUCE

1 large dill pickle, finely chopped

¼ cup finely chopped cucumber

¾ cup Mayonnaise (page 107)

Juice of ½ lemon

1 Tbsp chopped tarragon

1 Tbsp chopped parsley

½ tsp Worcestershire sauce

4 dashes TABASCO sauce

Sea salt and coarsely ground black pepper

Serves 4

CHICKPEA BATTER Put the chickpea flour in a skillet over low heat and gently toast for 2 to 3 minutes, until slightly browned. (Cooking out the raw flour gives it a nutty flavour.) Careful not to brown too much. In a bowl, combine the flour, water, and chili powder and mix well. Set aside.

TARTAR SAUCE Combine all the ingredients in a bowl and mix well. Taste and adjust seasoning, if desired. Refrigerate until use.

FISH Preheat oven to 140°F.

Pour the oil into a deep saucepan or deep fryer and heat over medium-high heat until it reaches a temperature of 365°F.

In a bowl, combine the fish and cilantro and toss. Dip the fish into the batter and carefully lower it into the hot oil, working in batches to avoid overcrowding. Using a slotted spoon, move the battered fish pieces around to prevent them from sticking to the sides or bottom of the pan and deep-fry for 5 to 8 minutes, or until they are crispy and begin to float.

Using a slotted spoon, transfer the fish to a plate lined with paper towels. Season with salt and pepper and keep warm in the oven at 175°F.

FRENCH FRIES

3 to 4 large russet or Kennebec potatoes

4 cups canola oil

1 tsp ground fennel seeds

Fine sea salt and coarsely ground black pepper

Extra-virgin olive oil, for drizzling

FRENCH FRIES Peel the potatoes, if desired, then cut into ¼-inch strips. Rinse for 3 to 5 minutes under cold running water until water runs clear. (This is to remove starch. Alternatively, the potato strips can be soaked overnight in a bowl of cold water in the fridge, then rinsed.)

Pour the oil into a deep fryer or deep saucepan and heat until it reaches a temperature of 330°F. Put the potatoes on a baking sheet and pat them dry with paper towels.

Carefully lower the potatoes into the hot oil, working in batches, if necessary, to avoid overcrowding. Fry for 5 minutes, or until softened. Transfer onto a baking sheet.

Increase the heat until the oil temperature reaches 375°F. Carefully lower potatoes back into the hot oil and brown for 5 to 7 minutes, until crispy and golden. Transfer to a bowl and toss with ground fennel, fine sea salt, and fresh ground black pepper. Drizzle with olive oil.

TO SERVE Serve the fried fish with chips and tartar sauce.

✛ Red Collar Brewing | Belgian Witbier | Kamloops
Brewed with Seville oranges and coriander, light and refreshing

Crab Cakes with Celery Root Slaw and Salsa Verde

I developed this crab cake while chef at the Wickaninnish Inn, on Vancouver Island, where fresh seafood is abundant. The secret to a great crab cake is the fish mousse. You're going to need a food processor, and you can use any kind of white fish. It's also perfect for a gluten-free diet because there aren't any breadcrumbs in this version.

CRAB CAKES

1 Tbsp grapeseed oil
3 Tbsp finely chopped onion
3 Tbsp finely chopped celery
3 Tbsp finely chopped fennel
6 oz cod, snapper, or any type of white fish
8 oz crabmeat
1 egg, beaten
¼ cup whipping (35%) cream
1 Tbsp chopped chervil or tarragon
2 Tbsp grapeseed oil or butter, for frying

SALSA VERDE

2 large dill pickles, coarsely chopped
2 tinned or jarred anchovies
3 cloves garlic
¼ cup extra-virgin olive oil
¼ cup chopped parsley
2 Tbsp chopped mint
1 Tbsp lemon juice
1½ Tbsp capers
1 tsp sambal oelek (see Note)

CELERY ROOT SLAW

¾ cup shredded celery root
3 Tbsp Mayonnaise (page 107)
½ Tbsp yellow or black mustard seeds

NOTE Sambal oelek is an Indonesian chili paste made with chilies, shrimp paste, fish sauce, garlic, ginger, shallot, green onion, palm sugar, lime juice, and vinegar. It can be found at Asian supermarkets.

Makes 4

CRAB CAKES In a small saucepan over medium heat, heat the 1 tablespoon oil, add the onions, celery, and fennel, and sauté for 2 to 3 minutes, until softened. (Do not brown.) Transfer to a bowl and chill in the fridge for 5 to 8 minutes.

Put the fish in the food processor and purée until smooth. Add the fish mousse to the onion mixture, stir in the crabmeat, egg, cream and chervil (or tarragon), and mix well. Divide the mixture into 4 equal portions and form into 1 ½-inch-thick patties. Place them on a plate and refrigerate until use.

SALSA VERDE Combine all ingredients in a food processor and pulse until mixed but still thick and chunky. Transfer to a bowl, cover, and chill in the fridge.

CELERY ROOT SLAW Combine all the ingredients and mix well.

TO ASSEMBLE In a nonstick pan over medium heat, heat the oil (or butter). Add the crab cakes and cook for 5 to 7 minutes, or until golden on one side. Flip over and cook for another 5 to 7 minutes, until cooked through. (Insert a skewer or knife into the centres. If it comes out hot, the crab cakes are ready.)

TO SERVE Spoon the salsa verde onto 2 plates and top each plate with 2 crab cakes. Garnish with celery root slaw and serve.

✦ **Mission Hill Family Estate** | **2014 Reserve Chardonnay** | **West Kelowna**
Crisp and delicious

Halibut Pastrami

This halibut dish is a nod to traditional pastrami flavours. Do note that it takes two days to prepare. The salt-cure process for this dish is quite similar to that of the Nordic salmon dish gravlax. It's a great way to serve a meaty fish like halibut, which holds up to the spices. The halibut pastrami can be wrapped and kept for up to two weeks.

INGREDIENTS

¼ cup kosher salt
¼ cup granulated sugar
¼ bunch parsley
½ bunch cilantro
1 large shallot, chopped
1 (1-lb) skinless halibut fillet
1 bay leaf
1½ Tbsp coriander seeds
1 Tbsp caraway seeds
1 Tbsp black peppercorns, cracked
1 tsp ground paprika
½ tsp chili flakes
2 Tbsp molasses

TO SERVE

Croutons
Mustard
Cornichons
Pickled vegetables
Caper berries

Serves 8

FIRST In a food processor, combine the salt, sugar, parsley, cilantro, and shallots and process until smooth. Generously coat the halibut with the mixture, until completely covered. Tightly wrap the halibut in several layers of plastic wrap. Place the fish on a plate and refrigerate for 12 hours. Flip the fish and cure for another 12 hours.

Remove the fish from the wrap and rinse off the curing mixture. (The halibut should be slightly firm to the touch.) Pat-dry with a paper towel and place on a small plate.

Combine the bay leaf, coriander and caraway seeds, peppercorns, paprika, and chili flakes in a small bowl and mix well. Warm the molasses slightly and brush it over the halibut until it's well coated on both sides. Press the spice mixture onto both sides of the fish, until it is completely coated. Refrigerate, uncovered, for 18 hours. The pastrami can be wrapped until use after this process.

TO SERVE Thinly slice the halibut pastrami and serve with croutons, mustard, cornichons, pickled vegetables, and caper berries.

Hot Smoked Salmon Fillets

You might not have a smoker at home, but a BBQ can do the job just as nicely. It might take a couple of tries to get it right, because there is an art to smoking. If you don't pay close attention you can over-smoke, and if you remove the meat too quickly, you can under-smoke. But the brining process, in itself, infuses the fish with flavour, making it tender and flaky once you've grilled it and the smoking process optional.

SALMON

2 cups water

1½ Tbsp coarse salt

3 Tbsp granulated sugar

3 Tbsp soy sauce

2 (2-inch) lemon peels

2 cloves garlic, chopped

1 shallot, chopped

1 (1½-lb) skinless salmon fillet

½ to 1 cup wood chips, such as apple or cherry

1 Tbsp olive oil, for frying

FINGERLING POTATO SALAD

1½ cups fingerling potatoes

6 radishes, sliced

1 small carrot, shredded or cut into thin strips

1 stalk celery, sliced diagonally

½ medium red bell pepper, seeded and chopped

½ medium yellow bell pepper, seeded and chopped

½ cup round cucumber slices

3 Tbsp sour cream

2 Tbsp balsamic vinegar

2 Tbsp capers

3 Tbsp chopped dill, plus extra for garnish

Serves 4

SALMON Bring the water to a boil in a medium pot, and then add the salt, sugar, soy sauce, lemon peels, garlic, and shallots. Bring to a boil again, reduce the heat to medium, and simmer for 5 minutes. Set aside to cool and then chill in the fridge for 60 to 90 minutes, until cold.

Pour the mixture into a large zip-top bag, add the salmon, and seal the bag. (Cut the salmon into smaller portions if desired.) Put the bag in the fridge and leave to brine for 4 to 6 hours. Remove the salmon from the brine, rinse under cold water, and pat-dry with a paper towel.

Preheat BBQ to medium. Place ½ cup of wood chips into a metal pan (or a disposable aluminum pan) and lightly sprinkle with water. Put the pan on top of the flame part of the BBQ, just under the rack, and leave to heat, until the wood chips start to smoke. (Adjust flame, if needed.) Put the salmon onto the grill rack over the smoking chips. Close the lid and smoke for 10 to 12 minutes, checking occasionally that the chips are still smoking. (Add more chips, if necessary.)

Transfer the salmon to a plate and extinguish the wood chips with water. Cut the salmon into portions if desired. *Continued overleaf*

FINGERLING POTATO SALAD Bring a medium saucepan of salted water to a boil over medium-high heat, add the potatoes, and cook for 20 to 25 minutes, or until tender. Drain and set aside to cool, then cut into small wedges.

Gently combine all the ingredients in a bowl and toss to coat. Set aside.

TO ASSEMBLE Heat the olive oil in a skillet over medium heat. Place the smoked salmon in the pan and pan-fry for 3 to 5 minutes, or until slightly brown. Flip over and cook for another 1 minute.

TO SERVE Transfer the potato salad to a serving platter. Put the salmon on top and serve immediately.

✦ **Silkscarf Winery** | **2015 Saignée Rosé** | **Summerland**
Produced from Malbec and Merlot grapes with minimum skin contact, this is a gorgeous salmon-coloured rosé with lots of fruit and acidity on the palate

Pasta and Bocconcini Bake

This is yet another case of refrigerator inspiration. I opened the door one day, found some leftover spaghettini, and threw this together. It was so good it's become one of my go-to favourites—crispy on the outside, melted cheesy goodness on the inside. The pasta bake can be made in advance and reheated. It's great for breakfast as well.

INGREDIENTS

250 g spaghettini or thin linguine

Sea salt and coarsely ground black pepper

3 Tbsp olive oil

½ medium red bell pepper, seeded and cut into strips

½ medium yellow bell pepper, seeded and cut into strips

½ medium green bell pepper, seeded and cut into strips

3 cloves garlic, chopped

10 button mushrooms, sliced

¼ cup chopped mixed herbs

3 Tbsp unsalted butter

6 slices prosciutto, cut into thin strips

1 cup tomato sauce

4 large bocconcini, thinly sliced

4 eggs, beaten

Serves 4 to 6

FIRST Bring a large saucepan of salted water to a boil over high heat, add the spaghettini (or linguine), and cook according to manufacturer's instructions. Drain, season with salt and pepper, and set aside.

Preheat oven to 400°F. Heat the oil in a 12-inch nonstick oven-proof pan or cast-iron skillet over medium-high heat. Add the peppers, garlic, and mushrooms, and sauté for 3 to 5 minutes until slightly cooked.

Add the herbs, toss, and transfer the mixture to a bowl. Return the pan to the stovetop and reduce the heat to medium-low. Add the butter and stir until melted. Add half the spaghettini (or linguine) and spread out to cover the bottom of the pan. Scatter the peppers and mushrooms on top, evenly distribute the prosciutto, and spoon over the tomato sauce. Place the sliced bocconcini on top to cover and then add the remaining spaghettini. Spread out and press down. Pour the eggs evenly over the mixture and bake for 10 minutes. Reduce the heat to 375°F and bake for another 15 to 20 minutes, until the pasta pulls away from the edges. Set aside to cool for 10 minutes.

TO SERVE Flip the pasta bake onto a platter. Cut into wedges and serve hot.

Sockeye Salmon BLT

This has been my long-time signature sandwich, from my days at the Pacific Palisades Hotel. The richness of the salmon is offset by the hint of licorice from the fennel seeds, the sweetness of the fig, and the saltiness of the pancetta. Fig-anise bread can be purchased from Terra Breads in specialty stores across B.C.

INGREDIENTS

4 slices pancetta

2 (4-oz) boneless and skinless sockeye salmon fillets

1 Tbsp fennel seeds, toasted and ground

4 slices fig-anise bread, toasted

2 medium lettuce leaves

1 medium tomato, sliced

MAYONNAISE

3 egg yolks, room temperature

1 Tbsp Dijon mustard

1 Tbsp white wine vinegar

Juice of ½ lemon

½ cup grapeseed oil

¼ cup olive oil

4 dashes Worcestershire sauce

Sea salt and coarsely ground black pepper

I've had revelatory moments with food throughout my career, such as early on, when I started making mayonnaise in culinary school. When I received an honorary degree in 2015, in my convocation address I told the little story of how the imposing instructor walked in wearing a white hat, white chef's coat, white pants, and white clogs and proceeded to teach us how to make mayonnaise. He took egg yolks, oil, mustard, and lemon and mixed them together—within minutes, he had mayonnaise. I was raised on mayonnaise that came out of a jar, and this new mayonnaise tasted totally different. It was a defining moment for me, when I understood what real food meant. I knew that I'd found my calling. Every home cook should try making his or her own mayonnaise at least once. And when you do, slather it on the Turkey and Nut Burger (page 108). The heavens will open.

Serves 2

MAYONNAISE In a mixing bowl, combine the egg yolks, mustard, vinegar, and lemon juice and whisk until combined. Gradually pour in the oils in a steady stream, whisking continuously and vigorously, until thickened. Add the Worcestershire sauce, and season to taste with salt and pepper. Transfer the mayonnaise to a container and refrigerate until use. It can be stored for up to 3 weeks. (Makes 1 cup.)

TO ASSEMBLE Heat a small skillet over medium heat, add the pancetta, and cook for 5 minutes. Flip over and cook for another 5 minutes, until browned and crispy. Set aside.

Preheat BBQ to medium heat, then place the salmon on the rack and grill for 3 to 5 minutes. Flip over and grill for another 2 to 4 minutes, or until just cooked through. (Alternatively, pan-fry for 5 to 8 minutes total over medium heat.)

Transfer ¼ cup of mayonnaise to a small bowl and stir in the ground fennel seeds. Generously spread the mayonnaise on the fig-anise toast. Lay the lettuce, pancetta, and tomato slices on one side. Top with a piece of salmon and close the sandwich with the other piece of toast.

TO SERVE Place the sandwiches on individual plates and serve immediately.

Turkey and Nut Burger

This turkey and nut burger is a light lunch alternative to a traditional burger, and it's been tweaked with unlikely flavour combos. Even I don't understand why this burger tastes so good. Yes, it has creamy Gruyère, herby cilantro, and hearty portobello mushrooms. Yes, soy sauce and chili paste add savoury Asian notes. However, the oddest ingredient in this burger has to be the peanut butter. Trust me on this one: it works.

INGREDIENTS

1½ lbs ground turkey

2 green onions, chopped

¼ cup finely chopped Gruyère

3 Tbsp peanut butter

2 Tbsp soy sauce

1 Tbsp sesame oil

1½ tsp chili paste, such as sambal oelek

2 Tbsp chopped cilantro

2 medium portobello mushrooms, cut into ½-inch-thick slices

2 Tbsp grapeseed oil

4 brioche burger buns

Mayonnaise (page 107)

Deli mix sprouts

French Fries (page 93), to serve

NOTE The turkey patties and mushrooms can be cooked in a pan on the stovetop as well. The turkey mixture can also be formed into small meatballs and pan-fried until cooked through. Serve with your favourite sauce and rice noodles.

Makes 4

FIRST Preheat BBQ to medium.

In a large bowl, combine the turkey, onions, cheese, peanut butter, soy sauce, sesame oil, chili paste, and cilantro and mix well. Shape into 4 equal-sized patties, 1 inch thick.

In a separate bowl, combine the mushrooms and oil and toss to coat.

Put the turkey patties on the grill, cook for 6 to 8 minutes, and flip over. Add the mushrooms and cook for another 6 to 8 minutes, until the internal temperature of the patties reaches 165°F.

Remove the mushrooms and the patties once cooked through. Place the buns, face side down, on the grill and toast for 30 seconds. Spread mayonnaise on both sides of the buns. Pile on the sprouts, and top each with mushrooms and a turkey patty. Top with the top halves of the buns.

TO SERVE Place the burgers on 4 individual plates, add a serving of fries to each, and serve immediately.

✚ Cannery Brewing | Naramata Nut Brown Ale | Penticton
Full bodied with a rich and gentle flavour

Grilled Flat Iron Steak Sandwich

Cooking with more economical cuts of meat is all the rage right now, which is a good thing, because those cuts have the best flavour. The flat iron steak is a cut from the top blade, just off the shoulder of the animal. Once the gristly membrane is removed, you have a well-marbled and richly flavoured steak. In this recipe, the flat iron is marinated for up to 24 hours, then grilled, and served in an open-face sandwich with pickled mushrooms and a hit of fresh, bitter radicchio.

INGREDIENTS

2 (6-oz) beef flat iron steaks, membrane removed (ask your butcher)

1 Tbsp grapeseed oil, for grilling

2 thick slices sourdough bread

1 Tbsp unsalted butter, for toasting (optional)

½ head radicchio leaves

Chips or a salad, to serve

STEAK MARINADE

1 small shallot, finely chopped

1 clove garlic, finely chopped

2 Tbsp red wine vinegar

1 Tbsp Dijon mustard

1 Tbsp soy sauce

1 Tbsp chopped mixed herbs

1 Tbsp brown sugar

PICKLED MUSHROOMS

3 Tbsp grapeseed oil (divided)

2 cups mixed mushrooms, such as button, cremini, shiitake, shimeji, and wild, cut into different shapes

¼ cup finely sliced leeks

1 clove garlic

½ tsp coriander seeds

1 tsp mustard seeds

Finely grated zest of ¼ lemon

2 Tbsp oregano leaves

1½ tsp granulated sugar

2 Tbsp white wine vinegar

Salt and freshly ground black pepper

Makes 2

STEAK MARINADE Combine the marinade ingredients in a zip-top bag, add steaks, and marinate in the fridge for 12 to 24 hours. Remove steaks from the bag and pat-dry with paper towels.

PICKLED MUSHROOMS In a large skillet set over medium-high heat, combine 2 tablespoons oil and the mushrooms and cook until just tender. Reduce the heat to low, add the remaining ingredients and the remaining 1 tablespoon oil, mix well, and cook for another 1 to 2 minutes. Transfer the mushrooms to a bowl and set aside to cool. (Makes 1 cup.)

TO ASSEMBLE Preheat BBQ to medium-high heat. Lightly oil the steaks and add them to the grill. Grill for 5 to 8 minutes, flip over, and cook for another 3 to 4 minutes, until medium rare. Transfer the steaks to a plate and set aside to rest for 3 to 5 minutes.

Butter one side of the bread slices, if desired. Put the slices on the BBQ, buttered side down, and grill for 30 to 45 seconds, until slightly charred.

Transfer the toasted bread to 2 plates. Top each slice with radicchio leaves and pickled mushrooms. Thinly slice the steaks and place on top of each sandwich.

TO SERVE Serve the sandwiches open face with chips or a salad.

✛ **Red Rooster Winery** | **2014 Merlot** | **Naramata**
Gorgeous red and black fruits, soft round tannins

Lemon Cheesecake Jars with Blueberry Compote and Shortbread

Refreshingly bright, this dinner-party dessert is perfect for serving year round: it makes for a tangy treat at a summer picnic as well as a bright palate cleanser after a heavy winter meal. It sees cheesecakes set in little Mason jars and topped with a tasty cookie crust. Your guests will love this pretty finish to their meal.

LEMON CHEESECAKE

500 g cream cheese, room temperature

½ cup granulated sugar

2 Tbsp all-purpose or gluten-free flour

2 eggs

1 tsp vanilla extract

Zest and juice of 2 lemons

Whipped cream, to serve (optional)

BLUEBERRY COMPOTE

1½ cups fresh or frozen blueberries, thawed if frozen

2 Tbsp granulated sugar

½ tsp cornstarch

1 Tbsp cold water

Makes 8 (4-fl oz) Mason jars

LEMON CHEESECAKE Preheat oven to 350°F. Put the cream cheese in a stand mixer using the paddle attachment and mix on low. Scrape down the sides of the bowl, and then pour in the sugar and flour. Mix well. Add the eggs, one at a time, scraping down the bowl after each addition. Add the vanilla and the lemon zest and juice.

Pour the mixture into 8 (4-fl oz) jars, three-quarters full. Place the jars in a deep casserole dish or roasting pan and fill with water until it comes halfway up the jars. Wrap the dish with foil and carefully place on the middle rack in the oven. Bake for 35 to 45 minutes, until the centres just begin to crack. Remove the jars from the water and place on a rack to cool. Refrigerate until needed.

BLUEBERRY COMPOTE In a small saucepan over medium heat, combine the blueberries and sugar and cook to a simmer.

In a small bowl, combine the cornstarch and water and mix well. Whisk the mixture into the pan and cook for 3 to 5 minutes, until thickened. Remove the compote from the heat, transfer to a bowl, and set aside to cool. *Continued overleaf*

SHORTBREAD

½ cup (1 stick) unsalted butter, softened

¼ cup granulated sugar, plus extra for dusting

1¼ cups all-purpose flour

SHORTBREAD In a bowl, cream together the butter and sugar. Add the flour and mix until the dough just comes together.

Lay plastic wrap on the counter, place the dough on top, and shape it into a log, about 2½ inches in diameter. Wrap tightly in plastic wrap and refrigerate for at least 1 hour.

Preheat oven to 325°F. Line a baking sheet with parchment paper.

Put the log on a cutting board, remove the plastic wrap, and slice into 8 to 12 cookies. Put them on the prepared baking sheet and lightly dust with sugar. Bake for 10 minutes, until the edges start to colour. Set aside to cool.

TO SERVE Spoon blueberry compote on top of each cheesecake, insert a cookie into the compote, and serve. Top with whipped cream, if using.

Apple Fritters

My World-Famous Pancakes batter (page 48) serves a dual purpose: this time as a golden fried fritter with creamy spiced apple purée. What's not to love? Make sure to use a large pot with plenty of room in case the oil bubbles up when frying.

INGREDIENTS

4 cups canola oil, for deep-frying

FRITTER BATTER

1¼ cups all-purpose flour

1 tsp baking powder

½ tsp baking soda

¼ tsp ground cinnamon

Pinch of salt

2 eggs

¾ cup plain yogurt

½ cup milk

1 tsp vanilla extract

3 medium Gala apples, unpeeled, cored and diced

CINNAMON SUGAR

½ cup granulated sugar

¼ tsp ground cinnamon

SPICED APPLE WHIPPED CREAM

2 medium McIntosh apples, cored, peeled, and diced

2 Tbsp brown sugar

½ tsp ground cinnamon

½ tsp ground allspice

1 tsp grated ginger

¼ cup water

1 cup whipping (35%) cream

1 to 2 Tbsp icing sugar

4 Tbsp sour cream

FRITTER BATTER Sift the flour, baking powder, baking soda, cinnamon, and salt into a medium bowl.

In a separate bowl, combine the wet ingredients and mix well. Pour the wet mixture into the dry mixture and mix well. Add the apples and stir. (The batter should be thick.)

CINNAMON SUGAR Combine the ingredients and mix well. Set aside.

SPICED APPLE WHIPPED CREAM In a small saucepan, combine the apples, brown sugar, cinnamon, allspice, ginger, and water and cook over medium heat for 8 to 10 minutes, until very soft. Transfer the mixture to a blender and purée until smooth. Transfer to a bowl and set aside to cool.

Whip the cream until medium peaks form, then add icing sugar and mix to stiff peaks. Gently fold sour cream and apple purée into whipped cream (to prevent the cream from deflating). Put it into an airtight container and refrigerate until required. The whipped cream can be stored in the fridge for up to 3 days. (Makes 2 cups.)

TO ASSEMBLE Pour the oil into a deep saucepan or deep fryer and heat over medium-high heat until it reaches a temperature of 350°F. Carefully lower spoonfuls of apple fritter batter into the oil, working in batches to avoid overcrowding. Using a slotted spoon, move the fritters around to prevent them from sticking to the sides or bottom of the pan. Deep-fry for 4 to 6 minutes, or until golden brown.

Using a slotted spoon, transfer the fritters to a plate lined with paper towels. Generously sprinkle the cinnamon sugar overtop.

TO SERVE Serve the fritters warm, with spiced apple whipped cream.

The Fudgesicle

As a kid, I used to visit my great aunt Minnie in Melfort, Saskatchewan, and she'd always make me chocolate frozen treats. This version is a nod to Minnie, and so chocolatey good that we serve it at the restaurant as part of our chocolate tasting plate. If you're looking for elevated crowd pleasers, try dipping the Fudgesicles into crunchy chocolate pearls, coconut, or cocoa powder immediately after removing them from the moulds.

INGREDIENTS

¾ cup milk

⅔ cup whipping (35%) cream

½ tsp vanilla extract

1 Tbsp gelatin powder

4 egg yolks

2 Tbsp granulated sugar

1 cup finely chopped good-quality dark chocolate

8 Popsicle sticks

Makes 8

FIRST In a small saucepan, combine the milk, cream, and vanilla and mix well. Add the gelatin powder, whisk, and then set aside for 5 minutes, until the gelatin blooms. Heat the mixture over medium heat until it reaches a simmer. Reduce the heat to medium-low and simmer for 5 minutes.

Place a pot of water on the stove and bring to a simmer over medium heat. In a heatproof bowl, combine the egg yolks and sugar and whisk together. Pour a little of the hot milk mixture into the eggs and whisk. Whisking continuously, slowly pour in the remaining milk. Place the bowl over the pot of simmering water and continuously stir, until the mixture has thickened and coats the back of a spoon.

Remove the bowl from the heat, add the chocolate, and stir until the chocolate is melted and incorporated. While still warm, pour into Popsicle moulds. Refrigerate for 30 minutes, until firm. Insert the Popsicle sticks and freeze for at least 4 hours.

TO SERVE Place the moulds in a bowl of warm water and pull on the Popsicle sticks—the Fudgesicles will slide out.

Dinnertime is that feast of a meal when you get to go all out, to show off your skills, to ramp up the flavours by refining your techniques.

FOR ME, AT HOME IN MY KITCHEN, it's that time of day when I let my creative juices flow. I really enjoy the planning and preparation that go into it. I even love the leftovers, especially braised meats that are often even better the next day, and which freeze so easily.

Many of the dishes here were inspired while I was cooking at home, after uncorking a bottle of good wine, and at my most relaxed. But you're still going to need some basic guidelines to make the process easier, so I'd like to share some tips to get you started. After all, God is in the details, as they say, and several of the dishes in this section depend on those little techniques or flavours to elevate them.

For example, searing food until it caramelizes is another great way to take the flavour up a notch. In the **Lamb Osso Buco [page 198]**, after searing the lamb, I add wine and stock to the pan with some herbs. As I stir these ingredients into the pan, I scrape off the caramelized meat bits—this is called deglazing the pan. In recipes, when I mention that you should look at the colour of the pan, I'm referring to that caramelization effect that we see in meats or veggies, when the sugars in the food start to brown, giving off a nutty flavour. We also see this method when we roast bones, for stock, or crab shells, as we do in one of my best-selling dishes, the luscious **Crab Cappuccino** [page 126].

Don't be intimidated by dishes that require some technique. They often just need more time to prepare. Risotto, for example, is all about paying attention. The final result should be loosy goosy on the plate, not moulded into a sticky dome. Unfortunately, many chefs outside of Italy don't realize this. I'll show you how to achieve the perfect risotto consistency in my recipe for **Pea, Sage, and Lemon Risotto** [page 153].

A good cook will find ways to boost flavours wherever and however they can. I stuff herbs under chicken skin in the **Slow-Grilled Chicken with Raspberry BBQ Sauce** [page 171] recipe. I use a more complex floral honey—instead of plain old honey—in the **Pan-Roasted Duck Breast with Heirloom Beets, Stone Fruits, Walnuts, and Wildflower-Lavender Honey** [page 177] dish. And I use orange zest to brighten up a hearty meal like **Bison Pot Roast with Smoked Paprika Butter and Crispy Kale** [page 189].

And in every dish, I am sure to use top-notch ingredients. When I ran the Pointe Restaurant at the Wickaninnish Inn, I'd make the most of Vancouver Island's bounty of off-the-boat seafood. It smelled so fresh it reminded me of the ocean air. I can't emphasize enough what an impact fresh, local food can have on your cooking. This means learning what separates the huge supermarket chain meats from the pasture-to-plate distributors who have lovingly raised free-range meat and hung it properly. It also means recognizing that those multicoloured, locally grown, chemical-free carrots just pulled out of the ground are going to be a zillion times more flavourful than the ones pulled off the refrigerator truck that travelled from somewhere far south two weeks ago.

There's another big bonus to learning how to extract the most flavour out of your food: cost. You won't feel the need to splurge on pricey cuts of meat when you learn how to transform a cheaper cut into something deeply succulent, or when you see how easy it is to make your own soup stock. And you'll no longer want to throw away your celery leaves or cheese rinds because you'll see them as flavour enhancers. It's an old-fashioned idea, making the most of your ingredients. In this section, I'll teach you how.

Cauliflower and Saffron Wedding Soup

I created this soup for the wedding of one of my chefs de cuisine, Robyn Sigurdson. I use a chunk of Parmigiano-Reggiano rind, which melts into the soup and gives it a rich, salty flavour, so this is a good reason to save those rinds. In a pinch, you can always use a grated version instead.

INGREDIENTS

2 Tbsp olive oil

¼ cup (½ stick) unsalted butter

4 cloves garlic, chopped

1 cup chopped leeks (about 1 small)

Generous pinch of saffron

3 cups chopped cauliflower (about 1 small head)

3 cups vegetable stock

1 cup whipping (35%) cream

1 cup chopped Parmigiano-Reggiano rinds (or shredded Parmigiano-Reggiano)

Sea salt and coarsely ground black pepper

Croutons, to serve (optional)

Good-quality extra-virgin olive oil, for drizzling

Serves 4

FIRST In a medium pot over medium heat, heat the oil and butter until melted. Add the garlic and leeks and cook for 2 to 3 minutes, until tender but without colour. (Reduce heat if it's too hot.) Add the saffron and cauliflower and stir, then cover and cook for 4 to 6 minutes until the cauliflower is slightly tender.

Add the stock, whipping cream, and Parmigiano-Reggiano and stir, then cover and cook on a low simmer for 25 to 30 minutes. Transfer the mixture, in batches, to a blender, and blend until very smooth. Strain through a fine-mesh strainer and season with salt and pepper to taste.

TO SERVE Ladle the soup into bowls, add croutons, if using, drizzle with extra-virgin olive oil, and serve.

Crab Cappuccino

My customers constantly ask for this recipe, and I've never given it out—until now. This is a tweaked version of the original at my restaurant, which would be too labour-intensive for the home cook. This immensely popular soup makes use of amazing West Coast Dungeness crab, which I usually bring in from Tofino. The frothed milk topping is a nod to the cappuccino, so we playfully serve it in a coffee cup—it's a showy and decadent way to start a meal.

INGREDIENTS

2 small Dungeness crabs

4 Tbsp grapeseed oil

¼ cup (½ stick) unsalted butter

1 small onion, chopped

1 stalk celery, chopped

¼ head fennel, chopped

8 button mushrooms, sliced

3 cloves garlic, chopped

¼ cup tomato paste

¼ cup all-purpose flour

6 cups vegetable stock

1 cup whipping (35%) cream

1 cup canned diced tomatoes

1 tsp black peppercorns

1 tsp fennel seeds

1 tsp yellow or black mustard seeds

4 bay leaves

Sea salt and black pepper

½ cup steamed milk, to garnish

Dried fish roe, to serve (optional)

Fried fennel fronds, to serve (optional)

Serves 4

FIRST Bring a large pot of salted water to a boil, add the crabs, and cook for 8 to 10 minutes. Drain and transfer the crabs to a bowl of ice water. When cool enough to handle, crack them open and discard the tomalley. Remove the crabmeat and set aside, reserving the shells. Break the shells into small pieces.

Heat a large pot over medium-high heat, add the oil and crab shells and cook for 7 to 10 minutes, until the shells turn slightly brown. Add the butter, onion, celery, fennel, mushrooms, and garlic and sauté for 5 to 8 minutes, until the bottom of the pot starts to colour. Use a wooden spoon to scrape it occasionally.

Add the tomato paste and cook for another 3 to 5 minutes. The bottom of the pot should take on a lot of colour. Scrape and stir. Add the flour, stir thoroughly, and cook for a minute. Add the stock, cream, diced tomatoes, peppercorns, fennel and mustard seeds, and bay leaves and mix well, scraping the bottom of the pot as much as possible. Reduce the heat to medium-low and simmer, partially covered, for 35 to 45 minutes. Strain carefully through a fine-mesh strainer and discard the shells and spices. Strain again into a pot, then taste and season as needed with salt and pepper. Reheat.

TO SERVE Use an electric mini whisk to froth the milk. Place the crabmeat in cups, ladle in the soup, and top with frothy milk. Garnish with dried fish roe and fried fennel fronds, if using.

✛ Road 13 Vineyards | **2015 Chip off the Old Block Chenin Blanc** | Oliver
Crisp, with key lime citrus and minerality

Side Stripe Prawns
and Gazpacho

In my part of the world, every spring turns to pandemonium as chefs make a mad rush for spot prawns, but my preference is the overlooked side stripe prawn. Wherever you live, find the freshest prawn you can for this summery dish served with a refreshingly light version of gazpacho.

INGREDIENTS

3 Tbsp extra-virgin olive oil, plus extra for drizzling

32 side stripe prawns, peeled and deveined

Seasonal salad greens

GAZPACHO

½ small red bell pepper, seeded and chopped

½ small yellow bell pepper, seeded and chopped

¼ small green bell pepper, seeded and chopped

4-inch cucumber, chopped

1 stalk celery, chopped

1 medium tomato, chopped

¼ small red onion, chopped

1 green onion, chopped

10 sprigs cilantro

2 Tbsp mint leaves

1 Tbsp tomato paste

2 tsp red wine vinegar

6 Tbsp tomato juice

Sea salt and coarsely ground black pepper

Serves 4

GAZPACHO Put the ingredients in a blender and purée until smooth. Use a fine-mesh strainer to strain the gazpacho into a bowl, season with salt and pepper to taste, and chill until needed. (Makes 2 cups.)

TO ASSEMBLE In a large skillet over medium-high heat, heat the oil, add the prawns (in batches if necessary, to avoid over-crowding), and sauté for 2 to 3 minutes until cooked through. Serve hot or chilled.

In a mixing bowl, toss the greens with a drizzle of olive oil.

TO SERVE Spoon the gazpacho onto 4 large plates, top with salad greens, and arrange 8 prawns atop each serving.

Fried Squash Blossoms Stuffed with Tomato Mascarpone

This dish is a contribution from my chef de cuisine Evelynn Braun, who was one of the top chefs on season four of Top Chef Canada. She's a rock star. These beautifully light appetizers are made from the blossoms of zucchini or other squash, which can be found at your local specialty produce shop (or better yet, grow your own). Due to their delicate nature, the blossoms should be cooked or eaten as soon as possible, but they can be stored in the refrigerator for a day or two.

INGREDIENTS

12 medium squash blossoms, such as zucchini blossoms

3 cups vegetable oil, for frying

TOMATO MASCARPONE

2 Tbsp extra-virgin olive oil

4 cloves garlic, crushed

2 medium shallots, sliced

3 medium ripe tomatoes, quartered

2 sprigs thyme

2 sprigs basil

2 sprigs parsley

Sea salt and coarsely ground black pepper

¾ cup mascarpone cheese

1 large egg yolk

¼ cup finely grated Parmigiano-Reggiano

¼ tsp dried Espelette pepper or chili flakes

Finely grated zest of ½ lemon

SQUASH BLOSSOMS

1 cup tempura flour

½ tsp salt

¾ cup club soda or sparkling water, chilled

Flaked sea salt (Maldon preferred)

Makes 12

TOMATO MASCARPONE Preheat oven to 400°F.

In an oven-safe heavy-bottomed saucepan over medium heat, heat the oil, then add the garlic, shallots, tomatoes, thyme, basil, and parsley and sauté 1 minute. Season with salt and pepper.

Transfer the tomato mixture to the oven and roast, uncovered, for 20 to 25 minutes until fully cooked and aromatic, stirring occasionally. Remove the thyme sprigs and transfer the mixture to a food processor or blender and process until smooth, thick, and pasty. Set aside to cool, and then chill in the fridge.

Put the mascarpone in a medium mixing bowl and, using a wooden spoon, whip until fluffy. Add the egg yolk, Parmigiano-Reggiano, Espelette pepper, and lemon zest. Gently fold in the chilled tomato purée and season to taste with salt and pepper.

Transfer to a piping bag. (Alternatively, fill a zip-top bag and cut the corner.) Set aside.

SQUASH BLOSSOMS In a mixing bowl, combine the tempura flour, salt, and club soda (or sparkling water) and mix well.

Preheat oven to 200°F. *Continued overleaf*

To prepare a squash blossom, gently rinse under cold water. Carefully open the petals, turn it upside down, and gently shake. Use your fingers to pick out and remove any pistil or stamen.

Carefully open a squash blossom and fill three-quarters of it with tomato mascarpone. Gently twist the end of the blossom to enclose the filling and repeat with the remaining blossoms. Refrigerate until needed.

Heat 2 inches of oil in a 10-inch heavy skillet over medium-high heat until it reaches a temperature of 375°F. Holding its base, dip a blossom into the batter to thinly coat, allowing excess batter to drip off. Repeat with 3 more blossoms. Carefully lower them into the hot oil and deep-fry for 2 to 3 minutes, until golden. Using a slotted spoon or tongs, gently transfer the blossoms to a tray lined with paper towels to drain. Repeat with the remaining blossoms, making sure that the oil returns to 375°F between batches. Keep fried blossoms warm in the oven while the others are frying.

TO SERVE Season the stuffed squash blossoms with flaked salt and serve immediately.

Brussels Sprouts Salad

When the temperature drops and you're looking to make the most out of cold-weather veggies, this delicious salad is a festive addition to holiday feasts, especially when served alongside roast chicken or beef. I use sweet Ambrosia apples, which are local, but use your own favourite regional apples. You want one with a good crisp bite.

INGREDIENTS

1 lb Brussels sprouts

2 Tbsp grapeseed oil

Sea salt and freshly ground black pepper

4 slices thick-cut bacon, cut into ¼-inch pieces

1 medium shallot, finely chopped

1 large Ambrosia apple (or any crisp apple), cored and cut into ½-inch wedges

3 Tbsp apple cider vinegar

1 Tbsp yellow or black mustard seeds

Serves 4

FIRST Preheat oven to 400°F.

Bring a small saucepan of water to a boil over high heat. Remove the outer few leaves of each Brussels sprout, add them to the water, and blanch for 15 seconds. Using a slotted spoon, transfer the leaves to a bowl of ice water to stop the cooking. (The leaves should be bright green.) Drain and set aside.

Put the Brussels sprouts into a large bowl, add the oil, and toss. Season with salt and pepper. Transfer to a baking sheet and roast for 15 minutes, until golden brown. Set aside and cool to room temperature.

Heat a skillet over medium heat, add the bacon, and cook for 4 to 6 minutes, or until almost crispy. Add shallots, reduce heat to medium-low, and cook for another 2 to 3 minutes. Add the apples and cook for another 3 to 4 minutes, until the apples are tender. Pour in the vinegar, stir in the mustard seeds, and toss. Add the roasted Brussels sprouts and gently stir the mixture to combine.

TO SERVE Transfer the salad to a serving platter or 4 individual bowls and garnish with the Brussels sprout leaves.

Turkey Wings

Who needs chicken wings when you can find turkey wings everywhere these days? This signature dish at micro bar • bites has a sweet-and-heat component, and is served with a traditional blue cheese dip. Because of their size, the wings are also a conversation stopper when they arrive at the table.

INGREDIENTS

½ medium onion, chopped

2 bay leaves

1 Tbsp salt

1 tsp black peppercorns

8 cups water

4 whole turkey wings, split into pieces

1 Tbsp grapeseed oil, for brushing

4 to 6 stalks celery, cut into 4-inch lengths, to serve

Lemon juice (optional)

Celery salt (optional)

BELIZEAN HOT SAUCE

1 small onion, chopped

1 carrot, chopped

6 cloves garlic, chopped

3 to 4 habanero chilies, chopped, seeds included

3 Tbsp apple cider vinegar

2 Tbsp honey

1 tsp coriander seeds

½ tsp ground allspice

½ tsp caraway seeds

½ tsp ground turmeric

Juice of 2 large limes

⅓ cup water

BLUE CHEESE SAUCE

2 oz blue cheese, crumbled

¼ cup sour cream

Serves 2 to 4

FIRST Put the onions, bay leaves, salt, peppercorns, and water in a large pot and bring to a boil over high heat. Add the wings and bring to a simmer, then cover, reduce heat to low, and cook for 1 hour, or until tender. Remove the wings and set aside to cool. Strain the broth and keep for another use. (It can be frozen and used to make soups, sauces, gravy, etc.)

BELIZEAN HOT SAUCE Combine all the ingredients in a pot and bring to a low boil. Reduce the heat to medium-low and simmer, covered, for 30 minutes. Transfer the mixture to a blender and blend until smooth. Pour the mixture into a container and refrigerate until needed. The hot sauce can be stored for up to 4 weeks. (Makes 1 ½ cups.)

BLUE CHEESE SAUCE Combine ingredients in a bowl and mix.

TO ASSEMBLE Preheat BBQ to medium heat. Brush the oil over the turkey wings, add to the grill, and grill for 8 to 12 minutes, turning occasionally, until crispy and coloured.

Toss the wings with just enough hot sauce to coat. Put the celery in a bowl, squeeze over the lemon juice and sprinkle with celery salt, if using.

TO SERVE Serve the wings on a platter with the seasoned celery and the bowl of blue cheese sauce.

+ Cannery Brewing | Lakeboat Lager | Penticton
Mellow malts and hops, crisp and refreshing

Chicken Confit Poutine

This dish takes a little extra time, but is totally worth the effort. At the restaurant, we make chicken leg confit in a small amount of duck fat using a sous-vide circulator. In this recipe, we have modified the process so you get similar results using plastic freezer bags. Poutine lovers go crazy for it.

INGREDIENTS

1½ cups Chicken Confit (recipe here)

8 to 10 cups French Fries (page 93)

1½ cups cheese curds, such as Village Cheese Co.'s Squeaky Cheese

1 to 2 cups Chicken Gravy (recipe here)

CHICKEN CONFIT

6 cloves garlic

3 sprigs rosemary

3 bay leaves

Small bunch thyme

3 Tbsp coarse salt

1 Tbsp black peppercorns

1 tsp juniper berries

3 chicken legs, split in half into thighs and drumsticks

½ cup duck fat

CHICKEN GRAVY

¼ cup grapeseed oil

1 lb chicken bones, preferably the neck, chopped

2 stalks celery, coarsely chopped

1 small onion, coarsely chopped

2 Tbsp tomato paste

¼ cup all-purpose flour

3 sprigs sage

Small bunch thyme

3 cups chicken stock

Sea salt and coarsely ground black pepper

Serves 6 to 8

CHICKEN CONFIT In a large bowl, combine the garlic, rosemary sprigs, bay leaves, bunch of thyme, salt, peppercorns, and juniper berries and mix well. Add the chicken legs and toss to mix. Cover with plastic wrap and refrigerate for 12 to 16 hours.

Preheat oven to 250°F. Rinse the legs under cold water for 5 minutes and discard the herb mixture. Pat-dry with a paper towel. Place the chicken in a large zip-top bag, spoon in the duck fat, and seal. Place the bag in another bag and ensure it's completely closed. Wrap the bag in a dishtowel and place in a deep ovenproof dish. (The towel keeps the bag submerged.)

Fill the dish with warm water, to two-thirds full, and cover with a lid or foil. Cook in the oven for 3 hours. (If not using it immediately, remove the towel and transfer the bag of confit to a bowl of ice water until cooled. Drain the water from the bowl and refrigerate until use.)

CHICKEN GRAVY Heat a medium pot over medium heat, add oil and chicken bones, and cook for 8 to 10 minutes, until very browned. Add the celery and onions and cook for another 3 to 5 minutes, until softened. Stir in the tomato paste and cook for another 2 minutes, scraping the bottom of the pot. *Continued overleaf*

Add the flour and stir for 1 minute, then add the sage, thyme, and chicken stock and mix well, scraping the bottom of the pot. Reduce to low heat and simmer for 30 to 45 minutes. Strain the gravy through a fine-mesh strainer into another pot and discard bones. Season the gravy with salt and pepper. Keep warm on the stove while you prepare the French Fries.

TO SERVE Remove the chicken from the bones and tear it into bite-sized pieces. Put the cooked fries in serving bowls, top with warm chicken confit and cheese curds, and ladle over the hot chicken gravy. Serve immediately.

NOTE This bagged process uses far less duck fat than the traditional method, and if you're feeling adventurous and prefer to cook by tradition, I encourage you to cook legs in a casserole dish completely covered with duck fat. The cooking time will be more or less the same, but you'll need far more duck fat! I like preparing the confit in advance, which allows it time to develop more flavour.

Root Vegetable Torte

This dish goes all the way back to my days working at the Chateau Whistler. It's a delicious way to pack all those winter root veggies into a single dish, and it's a long-time signature dish of mine. Alternating different colours of vegetables produces the greatest effect—a mandoline is an essential tool for making thin slices.

INGREDIENTS

Cooking spray

2 large carrots, thinly sliced

3 cloves garlic, finely chopped

3 large shallots, thinly sliced

½ cup shredded Parmigiano-Reggiano or cheese of your choice

1 cup whipping (35%) cream or vegetable stock

¼ cup chopped mixed herbs

Sea salt and coarsely ground black pepper

1 medium rutabaga, thinly sliced

2 medium white turnips, thinly sliced

6 medium sunchokes, thinly sliced (optional)

1 small celery root, thinly sliced

2 medium parsnips, thinly sliced

2 medium russet potatoes, thinly sliced

2 large red and/or gold beets, thinly sliced

3 oz mild chèvre (I like Happy Days Dairy's chèvre), crumbled, or ricotta cheese

NOTE This torte can be prepared the day before and chilled — simply reheat at 350°F. Or you can slice off individual portions and reheat.

Serves 4 to 6

FIRST Preheat oven to 400°F. Spray an 8-inch square casserole dish (or tart pan) with cooking spray. (Alternatively, line it with parchment paper.)

Layer the carrots in the bottom of the dish. Sprinkle with a little garlic, shallots, Parmigiano-Reggiano, cream (or stock), herbs, salt, and pepper. Repeat with the rutabaga, turnips, sunchokes, and all the remaining vegetables.

Sprinkle the goat cheese (or ricotta) on top and cover loosely with foil. Put the dish on a baking sheet and bake for 50 to 60 minutes, or until the centre of the torte feels tender when a fork is inserted. Remove from oven and let stand.

TO SERVE Serve the torte directly from the pan.

Eggplant and Summer Squash with Pan-Roasted Cauliflower Salad

Nothing speaks of summer like these eggplant and summer squash cutlets served with a roasted cauliflower salad on the side. This dish is super nutritious, packed with flavour, crispy golden, and lovely on the plate. The tender vegetables get texture from the panko coating, and the cauliflower salad is a crunchy contrast. The trick is to get the cutlets to the table while they're still hot and golden.

INGREDIENTS

1 large eggplant, cut into 1-inch-thick slices (4 in total)

1 medium zucchini, cut into 1-inch-thick rounds (6 in total)

¼ cup all-purpose flour

1 Tbsp chopped oregano

1 egg, whisked with 2 Tbsp water

¾ cup panko breadcrumbs

4 to 6 Tbsp olive oil, for frying

Sea salt and coarsely ground black pepper

PAN-ROASTED CAULIFLOWER SALAD

1½ cups cauliflower florets, cut into small pieces

3 Tbsp grapeseed oil

2 medium shallots, sliced

½ medium red bell pepper, seeded and cut into strips

2 Tbsp balsamic vinegar

2 Tbsp olive oil

2 Tbsp chopped parsley

1½ Tbsp chopped almonds

Finely grated zest of ½ lemon

Sea salt and coarsely ground black pepper

Serves 2

FIRST Spread out the eggplant and zucchini slices on a cutting board and place flour in a shallow bowl. Sprinkle oregano over the slices, and then dredge with flour. Pour the egg mixture into a large shallow bowl. Place the breadcrumbs on a large plate. Dip the eggplant and zucchini slices into the egg mixture, and then into the breadcrumbs. Set on a tray.

In a large skillet over medium heat, heat the oil, add the eggplants and zucchini, in batches if necessary, and pan-fry for 3 to 5 minutes until golden brown. Flip and pan-fry for another 2 to 4 minutes, until cooked through. Season with salt and pepper.

PAN-ROASTED CAULIFLOWER SALAD Heat a skillet over medium-high heat. Toss cauliflower in grapeseed oil, add to the skillet, and cook for 5 to 7 minutes, until browned. Add the shallots and peppers and cook for another 2 to 3 minutes, until softened. Remove from heat and set aside to cool. Transfer the mixture to a large bowl, add the remaining ingredients, and mix well. Season with salt and pepper to taste.

TO SERVE Arrange the eggplant and zucchini cutlets on 2 plates and top with cauliflower salad.

✛ vinAmité Cellars   2014 Cabernet Franc   Oliver
Lovely earthy notes with a hint of spice and cracked pepper

Pan-Fried Pasta

I learned this technique for cooking pasta from an Italian chef who
visited the kitchen back in the 1980s, when I worked for the Four Seasons.
The pasta is pan-fried and stock is added, a little at a time, risotto style.
The result is a delicious nuttiness that can't be beat, and it's my favourite
way of cooking pasta.

INGREDIENTS

⅓ cup olive oil

3 cups penne

1 onion, sliced

4 cloves garlic, chopped

1 Tbsp unsalted butter

3½ cups vegetable or chicken stock (divided)

2 cups spinach leaves

1 cup chopped kale

2 tomatoes, diced

¼ cup basil leaves, torn

¼ cup grated Parmigiano-Reggiano

Sea salt and coarsely ground black pepper

Serves 3 to 4

FIRST Heat a large pot over medium heat, add the olive oil and penne, and stir continuously for 3 to 5 minutes, until the noodles are golden on all sides (Careful not to brown too much—reduce heat if necessary.)

Add the onions, garlic, and butter and cook for 2 to 3 minutes, until the onions are softened. Add 1 cup of stock and cook until absorbed. Repeat until all the stock is absorbed and the pasta is cooked al dente. Add the spinach, kale, tomatoes, basil, and Parmigiano-Reggiano and stir for 1 to 2 minutes, until all the ingredients are heated through and the spinach and kale are wilted. Season with salt and pepper to taste.

TO SERVE Transfer the pasta to a serving platter, and serve immediately.

Parmesan Gnocchi with Broccoli Pistou

When word got out I was writing a cookbook, people started asking me if I'd be including the gnocchi recipe. Well, here it is. The trick to great potato gnocchi is in the handling of the potatoes. You want light, fluffy gnocchi, which starts with a potato ricer and lots of love. Do not over-handle the dough!

BROCCOLI PISTOU

6 cloves garlic

½ cup broccoli florets

1 cup arugula

¼ cup grated Parmigiano-Reggiano

¼ cup olive oil

Sea salt and coarsely ground black pepper

GNOCCHI

3 medium russet potatoes, peeled

2 egg yolks

½ cup grated Parmigiano-Reggiano, plus extra to garnish

2 cups all-purpose flour, plus extra for dusting

Sea salt and coarsely ground black pepper

Grapeseed oil, for greasing

2 to 3 Tbsp unsalted butter

NOTE The gnocchi can be prepared in advance and frozen. Once the gnocchi have been cut and placed on the baking sheet, freeze for 3 hours, until solid. Transfer the frozen gnocchi to a large zip-top bag and store for up to 1 month. When ready to use, boil from frozen.

Serves 3 to 4

BROCCOLI PISTOU Combine the garlic, broccoli, arugula, and Parmigiano-Reggiano in a food processor and blend until smooth. Gradually pour in the olive oil, until incorporated. Transfer to a bowl and season with salt and pepper. Set aside.

GNOCCHI Preheat oven to 375°F.

Put the potatoes on a baking sheet and bake for 1 hour, or until softened. Remove skin, then cut the potatoes in half, lengthwise. While still hot, press the pieces through a potato ricer into a bowl. (Ricing allows for more volume and adds fluffiness to it. Alternatively, you can coarsely grate.)

Add the egg yolks and Parmigiano-Reggiano and stir to mix well. Refrigerate for 30 minutes to cool.

Turn out the mixture onto a floured surface and, using your hands or a pastry scraper, combine the flour with the potato mixture, until fully incorporated.

Bring a pot of salted water to a boil over high heat, drop a small piece of dough into the water, and once it floats to the surface, taste to make sure it's firm. (If it's too soft, add more flour to the mixture.) Season the dough with salt and pepper to taste. *Continued overleaf*

Line a baking sheet with parchment paper. Divide the dough in half. Roll one portion into a log, about ½ inch in diameter, and cut into 1-inch pieces. Repeat with the other half. Put the gnocchi on the prepared baking sheet.

Grease another baking sheet. Return the pot of salted water to a boil, add the gnocchi, in batches if necessary, and blanch for 4 to 6 minutes, until they float. Using a slotted spoon, transfer the gnocchi to the greased baking sheet and let cool.

Heat a nonstick skillet over medium heat, add the butter and the gnocchi, and pan-fry for 8 to 10 minutes, until golden brown.

TO SERVE Spoon the pistou over the cooked gnocchi and mix well, then divide between 3 to 4 plates, and serve immediately.

+ Amante Picante cocktail [page 217]
Reposado tequila, cucumber, cilantro, and lime

Pea, Sage, and Lemon Risotto

I'm a little bit obsessive about the proper cooking of risotto. True risotto does not get its creamy consistency from the addition of cream or butter. Instead, it comes from good-quality rice, the stock, and a good dose of patience. I've watched great Italian chefs make risotto, and it truly is a labour of love. You cannot rush it. It's the cooking process at its finest—transforming something as mundane as rice into a decadent main course.

INGREDIENTS

¼ cup olive oil

1 small onion, finely chopped

4 cloves garlic, finely chopped

1 cup carnaroli rice

3 ½ cups vegetable stock (divided)

½ cup grated Parmigiano-Reggiano

1 cup peas, thawed if frozen

2 Tbsp unsalted butter

1 tsp finely grated lemon zest

5 sage leaves, chopped

Sea salt and coarsely ground black pepper

Serves 4

FIRST Heat a medium pot over medium heat, pour in the oil and tilt to coat the bottom of the pot, and add the onions and garlic. Sauté and cook for 2 to 3 minutes, until softened but not coloured (reduce heat if necessary). Add the rice and stir for 1 minute. Add ½ cup stock and stir frequently for 3 minutes, or until most of the stock has been absorbed. Add another ½ cup stock and repeat until the rice is cooked al dente. (It should be somewhat loose in consistency but not firm nor soupy.)

Reduce heat to low, gently stir in the remaining ingredients, and mix well. Season to taste with salt and pepper.

TO SERVE Transfer the risotto to a serving platter, and serve immediately.

Oat-Crusted Arctic Char

When you're camping and you catch a fish, chances are good you've got
oats or cornflakes or some kind of crunchy cereal on hand. I call this a refined
campfire dish. My customers think there's a big secret to making this dish,
but it's one of my simplest menu items and our number-one seller.

INGREDIENTS

2 slices pancetta

1 Tbsp grapeseed oil

2 (5- to 6-oz) pieces skinless Arctic char (see Note)

Sea salt and coarsely ground black pepper

⅓ cup steel-cut or rolled oats

2 Tbsp olive oil

4 Tbsp unsalted butter

Juice of 1 lemon

2 Tbsp maple syrup

1 Tbsp chopped parsley

1 tsp chopped chives

Balsamic reduction, for drizzling

Cooked nugget potatoes, wilted spinach, and seasonal vegetables, to serve

NOTE This recipe can be adapted to use thinly pounded chicken breast or boneless pork loin instead of Arctic char.

Serves 2

FIRST Heat a small skillet over medium heat, add the pancetta, and cook for 5 minutes. Flip over and cook for another 5 minutes, until browned and crispy. Set aside.

Heat a skillet over medium-high heat. Rub the grapeseed oil on the char and season with salt and pepper. Press the oats onto both sides of the fish, until coated. Add the olive oil and butter to the hot pan, add the char, and cook for 3 to 4 minutes, until golden brown. Flip over and cook for another 2 to 4 minutes, or until cooked through. Transfer the char to 2 plates.

Continue to heat the butter mixture in the pan over medium-high heat until it begins to brown. Add the lemon juice, maple syrup, parsley, and chives and mix well.

TO SERVE Pour the sauce over the cooked char. Garnish with pancetta, drizzle with balsamic reduction, and serve with potatoes, wilted spinach, and seasonal vegetables.

+ **Liquidity Wines** | **2015 Viognier** | **Okanagan Falls**
Earthy spice with fresh acidity and savoury notes

Prosciutto-Wrapped Ling Cod

You can make the ragout ahead of time and prepare the fish and all the other ingredients quickly. It's a straightforward, fresh, simple fish dish that gets a flavour boost from the prosciutto and basil.

120 g bucatini or other long pasta, such as spaghetti, linguine, or fettuccine

Sea salt and coarsely ground black pepper

2 (5- to 6-oz) pieces skinless ling cod

2 basil leaves

2 large slices prosciutto

1 Tbsp unsalted butter

Parmigiano-Reggiano, for sprinkling (optional)

Olive oil, for drizzling

RAGOUT

¼ cup olive oil

Micro greens, to garnish (optional)

½ medium red onion, finely chopped

½ cup finely chopped butternut squash

½ cup finely chopped eggplant

½ cup canned crushed tomatoes

1 Tbsp chopped oregano

1 Tbsp chopped parsley

1 tsp thyme leaves

Sea salt and pepper

Serves 2

RAGOUT In a saucepan over medium-high heat, heat the oil. Add the onions, squash, and eggplant, stir, and cook for 5 to 8 minutes, until tender. Add the remaining ingredients, stir, and cook for another 3 to 5 minutes, until hot. Season with salt and pepper to taste. Keep warm on the stove.

NEXT Bring a large saucepan of salted water to a boil over high heat, add the bucatini (or other pasta), and cook according to manufacturer's instructions. Drain, season with salt and pepper, and set aside in the cooking pot with the lid on.

Season ling cod fillets with pepper and top each piece with 1 basil leaf. Wrap a slice of prosciutto around each piece.

In a nonstick skillet over medium heat, melt the butter, add the fish, and pan-fry for 3 to 5 minutes, until lightly browned. Flip the fish and cook for another 2 to 3 minutes, until cooked through.

TO SERVE Spoon the ragout onto 2 plates, place pasta over the sauce, and top with a piece of ling cod. Sprinkle the Parmigiano-Reggiano overtop, if desired, and a drizzle of olive oil. Serve.

Mussels and Clams

This is my not-so-classic mussels and clams, with the spicy addition of chorizo. Serve with a good chunk of bread to soak up the broth. It's okay if your shellfish only open a little, but toss the ones that stay shut.

INGREDIENTS

1 lb mussels, rinsed in cold water

1 lb clams, rinsed in cold water

2 Tbsp olive oil

2 medium shallots, sliced

4 cloves garlic, chopped

1 fresh chorizo sausage, chopped

⅓ cup chicken stock

1 medium tomato, chopped

5 basil leaves, chopped

1 Tbsp chopped parsley

¼ cup peas, thawed if frozen

1 baguette, to serve

Serves 2 (mains) or 4 (appetizers)

FIRST Tap the mussels and clams. If they do not close, discard.

In a large pot over medium-high heat, heat the oil, add the shallots, garlic, and chorizo, and stir. Sauté for 3 to 5 minutes, until the sausage is slightly crispy. Add the mussels and clams, stir, and cook for another minute. Add the chicken stock, cover, and cook for 4 to 6 minutes, until the shells have opened. Discard any shells that don't. Add the tomato, basil, parsley, and peas, stir, and cook for another 1 minute, until warmed through.

TO SERVE Transfer the mussels and clams into individual bowls and divide the liquid between them. Serve with the baguette, which can be torn and dipped into the broth.

+ BNA Brewing   Don't Lose Your Dinosaur IPA   Kelowna
Bold ale, soft citrus, and smooth finish

The RJB

This top-selling dish was named after me because I absolutely love this steak sandwich. The bacon, brioche, and crab are amazing. Take the time to properly caramelize the onions, because that sweetness is a key component to the flavour profile. Our onion jam goes back to our Fresco days, and it was massively popular.

INGREDIENTS

2 (5-oz) beef tenderloin steaks

2 brioche buns, halved lengthwise

2 Tbsp Mayonnaise (page 107)

¼ cup Caramelized Onion Jam (recipe here)

2 oz crabmeat, warmed in 1 Tbsp melted butter

1 oz Tyrolean-style cured bacon (I prefer Sedo's) or prosciutto

Roasted potatoes and roasted whole mushrooms, to serve

CARAMELIZED ONION JAM

½ cup grapeseed oil

½ cup (1 stick) unsalted butter

1 medium white onion, sliced

1 medium red onion, sliced

1 medium sweet onion, such as Vidalia or Walla Walla, sliced

2 medium shallots, chopped

½ medium leek, sliced

8 cloves garlic, chopped

⅓ cup brown sugar

1 tsp ground allspice

¼ cup balsamic vinegar

3 Tbsp chopped parsley

Sea salt and coarsely ground black pepper

NOTE At RauDZ, we serve the potatoes with house-made duck fat mayonnaise for extra decadence, but you can serve them with your favourite condiment.

Makes 2

CARAMELIZED ONION JAM Heat a large pot over medium heat and add the oil and butter. When the butter has melted, add the onions, shallots, leeks, and garlic and sauté for 15 to 20 minutes, until caramelized. (Adjust heat if necessary to prevent burning.)

Add the sugar, allspice, and vinegar, reduce the heat to low, and cook for another 10 minutes. Transfer the mixture to a food processor and process until evenly chopped and slightly chunky. Transfer the mixture to a bowl, add the parsley, and season to taste with salt and pepper. Refrigerate until needed. (Makes 3 cups. Extra can be kept in fridge for up to 7 days or canned in jars.)

TO ASSEMBLE Preheat BBQ to medium-high heat. Grill the steaks for 5 to 7 minutes, flip over, and cook for 4 to 6 minutes, until medium rare. (Alternatively, pan-fry the steaks over medium-high heat for 5 to 7 minutes on each side.) Transfer the steaks to a plate and set aside to rest for 3 to 5 minutes.

Place the buns, face side down, on the grill and toast.

Spread the mayonnaise on the bottom half of each bun and onion jam on the other. Drain some of the butter from the warmed crabmeat, and spoon the crabmeat on one side of the brioche. Add the beef and then the Tyrolean-style cured bacon (or prosciutto). Close the bun.

TO SERVE Place the steak sandwiches on individual plates. Serve with roasted potatoes and roasted whole mushrooms.

✛ **Painted Rock Estate Winery** | **2014 Red Icon** | **Penticton**
Blend of Merlot, Cabernet Franc, Malbec, Petit Verdot, and Cabernet Sauvignon. Velvety tannins and high acid, bold, and weighty

Steelhead Trout with Wild Mushroom Crust and Sautéed Mushrooms

Wild mushrooms add an earthy umami flavour to the crust, which pairs nicely with the delicate trout (a member of the salmon family). If you don't have a food processor, the dried mushrooms can be ground in a coffee grinder. To clean out the coffee grinds, throw in a little chunk of bread and grind that first. This is an excellent opportunity to make use of the abundance of mushrooms available at most farmers' markets in the fall.

INGREDIENTS

1 oz dried wild mushrooms

1 Tbsp grapeseed oil

2 (6-oz) skinless steelhead trout fillets, each cut into 2 pieces

2 Tbsp olive oil

3 Tbsp unsalted butter

2 cloves garlic, finely chopped

1 medium shallot, sliced

2 to 3 cups assorted mushrooms (I like shiitake, chanterelles, shimeji, porcini), roughly chopped

¼ cup whipping (35%) cream

2 Tbsp brandy

1 Tbsp chopped tarragon

1 tsp whole pink peppercorns

2 to 4 heads baby bok choy, steamed or sautéed, to serve

Serves 2

FIRST Put the wild mushrooms in a food processor or a clean coffee grinder, and process until finely ground.

Rub the grapeseed oil over the fillets and season with salt and pepper. Sprinkle the ground mushroom on the flesh side of the fillets and press into the fish. In a skillet over medium heat, heat the olive oil, and add the fillets, mushroom side down. Cook for 3 to 4 minutes, until golden brown. Flip and cook for another 2 to 4 minutes, until cooked through. Remove fish from the pan and keep warm in the oven at 175°F.

Put the butter in the same pan and melt over medium to high heat. Add the garlic and shallots and cook for 1 minute, until slightly soft. Add the mushrooms and sauté for 4 to 6 minutes, until tender. Add the remaining ingredients and cook for 2 to 3 minutes until the cream has slightly thickened. (Increase heat if necessary.) Season to taste with salt and pepper.

TO SERVE Divide the mushrooms between 2 plates and place steelhead pieces on top. Serve with baby bok choy.

Haida Gwaii Halibut and Asparagus

This dish is a nod to spring when both spring halibut and tender asparagus are in season. I finish it with an egg, bacon, and pickle topping, which adds texture and a hit of flavour, is super easy to make, and is a nice change from sauce.

INGREDIENTS

1 lb asparagus, tough stalk ends removed

4 Tbsp unsalted butter

1 (12-oz) skinless halibut fillet, cut in half

Sea salt and coarsely ground black pepper

2 cloves garlic, thinly sliced

EGG-PICKLE MIXTURE

2 eggs

2 slices bacon, chopped

1 large dill pickle, chopped

1 Tbsp chopped parsley

1 Tbsp extra-virgin olive oil

Serves 2

EGG-PICKLE MIXTURE Put the eggs in a small saucepan, add enough cold water to cover by 1 inch, and bring to a boil over medium-high heat. Cover, remove from heat, and set aside 8 to 10 minutes. Drain, then cool in cold water. Peel, slice, and set aside.

Heat a small skillet over medium heat, add the bacon, and sauté for 5 minutes, until crispy. Set aside.

Combine all ingredients in a small bowl. Keep at room temperature before serving.

TO ASSEMBLE Using a steamer, steam asparagus for 4 to 6 minutes, until just tender.

Meanwhile, heat a nonstick skillet over medium heat and add the butter. Season the halibut with salt and pepper, add it to the pan, and cook for 4 to 6 minutes, until golden. (Adjust heat of pan higher or lower if necessary.) Add the garlic to the pan. Flip the halibut pieces over and cook for another 2 to 4 minutes, until cooked but still slightly translucent in the centre. Transfer the fish to a plate and set aside.

TO SERVE Put the asparagus on 2 serving plates, spoon over the egg-pickle mixture, and place the halibut on top. Spoon over garlic pan juices and serve.

✚ **Checkmate Artisanal Winery**   **2013 Queen Taken Chardonnay**   **Oliver**
Citrus peel and white peaches, rich with a long finish

Bamboo Steamed Fish
in Curry

Curry is all about the layering of flavours, and this dish is all about the curry sauce. If you take the time to prepare the curry properly and to understand the nuances, you'll never buy pre-mixed curry powders again. Best of all, this recipe makes four cups, which means half of it can be reserved for another use.

INGREDIENTS

1 (12-oz) piece skinless snapper, cod, or halibut

Sea salt

Cooking spray

2 cups Curry Sauce (recipe here)

Cooked basmati rice or other grains, to serve

½ cucumber, sliced, to serve

CURRY SAUCE

5 cloves

½ Tbsp ground cumin

½ tsp black peppercorns

½ tsp coriander seeds

1 large onion, chopped

4 cloves garlic

2 Tbsp chopped ginger

½ bunch cilantro

¼ cup grapeseed oil

1 tsp ground paprika

1 tsp ground turmeric

1 (5.5-fl oz) can tomato paste

2 cups canned crushed tomatoes

1½ tsp ground tamarind

½ tsp chili flakes

1 Tbsp white wine vinegar

2 Tbsp granulated sugar

1 (14-fl oz) can coconut milk

Sea salt

Serves 2 to 4

CURRY SAUCE Combine the cloves, cumin, peppercorns, and coriander seeds in a small skillet over medium-low heat and toast for 1 to 2 minutes until fragrant, shaking the pan occasionally to prevent burning. Transfer to a mortar and pestle or a spice grinder and grind. Set aside.

Place onions, garlic, ginger, and cilantro in a food processor and purée until smooth.

In a medium pot over medium heat, add the oil and the onion mixture and cook for 8 to 10 minutes, stirring continuously, until it takes on colour and begins to stick to the bottom. (Take care as it may splatter.) Add the toasted spices, paprika, and turmeric, and cook for another 2 to 3 minutes, scraping the bottom of the pan to prevent burning.

Stir in the tomato paste and cook for 1 minute. Add the remaining ingredients and stir well, scraping the bottom of the pot. Cover, reduce heat to medium-low, and gently simmer for 25 to 35 minutes. Stir occasionally.

Transfer the sauce to a blender and purée until smooth, if desired. (Sauce can also be left as is.) Season with salt to taste. (Makes 4 cups. Extra sauce can be refrigerated for up to 5 days or frozen for 1 month. To serve, simply thaw and reheat.)

To boost flavour, we chefs have a few tricks up our sleeves. For example, heat is a great way to add flavour, so I give my peppercorns a quick toast in my cast-iron pan before they go into the grinder. I toast coriander seeds, pumpkin seeds, almonds, peanuts, sesame seeds, cinnamon sticks—you name it.

TO ASSEMBLE Add 2 inches of water to a pot or large skillet and bring to a simmer over medium heat. Season the fish with salt. Spray a bamboo steamer (or steamer basket) with cooking spray, add the fish, and set on top of the pot (or in the skillet). Put the lid on and steam the fish for 4 to 6 minutes, until cooked through but still slightly translucent.

TO SERVE Transfer the fish to a serving platter, generously ladle over the curry sauce, and serve with rice (or grains) and cucumber slices.

✚ **Lake Breeze Vineyards** | **2015 The Spice Jar** | **Naramata**
A fruity blend of Gewürztraminer, Ehrenfelser, Viognier, and Schönberger

Slow-Grilled Chicken with Raspberry BBQ Sauce

People are often too intimidated to barbecue chicken because they might burn the heck out of it. It needs to be cooked low and slow, on the lowest setting possible on the BBQ, so the meat is moist and fork tender. The tangy Raspberry BBQ Sauce is the perfect accompaniment for that smoky meat.

INGREDIENTS

1 (2½-lb) free-range chicken (I prefer Sterling Springs in Falkland)

¾ cup chopped mixed herbs

2 Tbsp olive oil

Sea salt and coarsely ground black pepper

2 cups Raspberry BBQ Sauce (recipe here)

RASPBERRY BBQ SAUCE

2 Tbsp grapeseed oil

1 medium onion, chopped

3 cloves garlic, chopped

1 Tbsp finely chopped ginger

1½ cups raspberries

¼ cup tomato paste

⅓ cup canned tomatoes

¼ cup brown sugar

2 Tbsp raspberry vinegar (can be found at specialty grocery stores; I like the Vinegar Lady's)

2 Tbsp molasses

1 tsp Worcestershire sauce

1 tsp ground cumin

1 tsp dry mustard

½ tsp ground paprika

½ tsp ground allspice

¼ tsp black pepper

Juice of 1 orange

Serves 4

RASPBERRY BBQ SAUCE In a medium pot over medium heat, combine the oil, onions, garlic, and ginger and sauté for 2 to 3 minutes until soft. Add the remaining ingredients and stir to mix well. Cover, reduce to low heat, and cook for 30 minutes. Transfer the mixture to a blender and blend until smooth. Transfer to a bowl and set aside to cool, then cover and refrigerate until needed. The sauce will keep up to 4 weeks. (Makes 2 cups.)

CHICKEN Preheat BBQ on low heat.

Using a pair of kitchen scissors, cut the chicken, through the ribs, along one side of the backbone. Repeat along the other side. Remove the backbone if you like (it can be used to make stock), but it's not necessary. Place the chicken on a cutting board, breast side up, and flatten with the heel of your hand. (Alternatively, ask your butcher to do this.)

Using your fingers, carefully loosen the skin of the breasts and legs, taking care not to break the skin. Stuff the herbs under the skin and spread out to evenly distribute. Rub the chicken with oil and season with salt and pepper. *Continued overleaf*

GRILLED VEGETABLES

2 medium bell peppers, seeded and cut into large chunks

1 medium eggplant, cut into large chunks

1 medium zucchini, cut into chunks

Handful of green beans, trimmed

2 cobs of corn, halved

2 Tbsp olive oil

2 Tbsp balsamic vinegar

Sea salt and coarsely ground black pepper

Place the chicken, cut side down, on the BBQ rack and cook for 45 minutes. (Do not turn over, but adjust on the rack if there are any flare ups.)

In a large bowl, combine all of the grilled vegetables ingredients, then add the vegetables to the grill. Generously brush the chicken with BBQ sauce and cook for another 15 minutes, until cooked through and the chicken reaches an internal temperature of 165°F at the thigh. Turn the vegetables a few times to grill on all sides and avoid burning. Add more sauce to the chicken, as desired.

TO SERVE Transfer the chicken to a serving platter and surround with the grilled vegetables. Serve family style.

+ **50th Parallel Estate** | **2013 Pinot Noir** | **Lake Country**
Soft and silky, with lots of raspberry fruit and a long finish

Honey and Coffee–Glazed Quail

Quail is a small game bird with dark, delicate meat and requires little cooking time, so be very careful not to overcook it (which causes it to be tough and dry). And use this opportunity to roast some radishes: chefs like to roast radishes because they get a subtle nutty flavour when cooked.

INGREDIENTS

1½ cups very strong brewed coffee

¼ cup brown sugar

2 Tbsp coarse salt

1 Tbsp grated ginger

1 tsp coriander seeds

4 to 8 semi-boneless quails, 1 to 2 per person depending on size (see Note)

16 to 24 radishes, tops removed

2 Tbsp olive oil

1 Tbsp yellow or black mustard seeds

Coarsely ground black pepper

Dressed salad leaves, to serve (optional)

HONEY-COFFEE GLAZE

¼ cup honey

1 tsp fine-ground coffee

¼ tsp ground cinnamon

Pinch of chili flakes

1 Tbsp chopped cilantro

¼ tsp coriander seeds, coarsely ground

NOTE If you can't find semi-boneless quail, you can do it at home. Using a pair of kitchen scissors, cut the quail, through the ribs, along one side of the backbone. Repeat along the other side. Place the quail on a cutting board, breast side up, and flatten with the heel of your hand. (Alternatively, ask your butcher to do this.)

Serves 4

FIRST Combine the coffee, sugar, salt, ginger, and coriander seeds in a pot, stir to mix, and heat over medium heat, until the salt and sugar are dissolved. Set aside to cool.

Place quails in a large zip-top bag (the quails will all fit in one bag) and cover with coffee brine. Put in the fridge and brine for 3 to 4 hours. Rinse under cold water and then pat-dry with paper towels.

HONEY-COFFEE GLAZE Combine all ingredients in a small pot and heat over low heat for 5 to 8 minutes. Set aside.

TO ASSEMBLE Preheat oven to 400°F.

Put the radishes in a small roasting pan, add the oil and mustard seeds, and toss. Roast for 20 to 30 minutes, until slightly brown and cooked through. Season with salt and pepper. Set aside.

Preheat BBQ to high heat. Put the quail on the grill, cut side down, and cook for 6 minutes, flip over, and cook for another 2 minutes, until cooked through. (Overcooking will toughen the meat.)

TO SERVE Thinly slice 4 radishes. Transfer the quail to a serving platter, drizzle over the honey-coffee glaze, and serve with whole and sliced radishes (and dressed salad, if using).

Pan-Roasted Duck Breast with Heirloom Beets, Stone Fruits, Walnuts, and Wildflower-Lavender Honey

In 2015, when our executive chef Brock Bowes won Chopped Canada, and donated a big chunk of his prize money to a local charity, it made me pretty proud to have him leading our team. He contributed this dish to the book. Rich, fatty duck meat always goes well with anything sweet, and here it is paired with stone fruits and good honey.

INGREDIENTS

4 boneless skin-on duck breasts

¼ cup walnuts, toasted

2 to 3 peaches, apricots, and/or nectarines, pitted and cut into wedges

¼ cup wildflower-lavender honey (recipe here)

BRINE

2 cups water

¼ cup kosher salt

½ cup unpacked brown sugar

1 medium shallot, chopped

2 bay leaves

1 tsp black peppercorns

HEIRLOOM BEETS

2 cups kosher salt

4 to 6 mixed heirloom beets, such as red, gold, and striped, washed and trimmed

WILDFLOWER-LAVENDER HONEY

¼ cup wildflower honey

2 sprigs lavender

Serves 4

BRINE Combine all ingredients in a pot and bring to a boil. Reduce the heat and simmer for 10 minutes. Transfer to a large bowl and set aside to cool.

Score the skin of each duck breast. (Do not cut through the meat.) Place the duck in the brine, submerge, and cover with plastic wrap (or transfer to a zip-top bag). Brine in the fridge for 14 to 18 hours.

Rinse the duck under cold running water and pat-dry with paper towels. Set aside.

HEIRLOOM BEETS Preheat oven to 350°F.

Put the salt in a small casserole dish and spread it out to cover the bottom. Place the beets on top, cover the pan with foil, and roast for 1 hour, until they can be easily pierced with a knife. Uncover and let cool, then peel and set aside.

WILDFLOWER-LAVENDER HONEY Combine the honey and lavender in a pot and heat for 5 minutes over low heat. Let steep for 10 minutes, then remove the lavender. *Continued overleaf*

TO ASSEMBLE Heat a large skillet over medium heat, add the duck breasts, skin side down, and cook for 10 to 12 minutes, until fat renders and skin is slightly crispy. Flip over and cook for 4 to 6 minutes, for medium rare. Transfer the duck to a plate and set aside to rest for 5 minutes.

Slice the duck breasts and arrange the pieces on 4 plates. Arrange the beets (cutting the larger ones into slices or wedges), walnuts, and fruit wedges around the duck.

TO SERVE Drizzle a tablespoon of honey over each dish and serve.

+ Quails' Gate Estate Winery | **2014 Stewart Family Reserve Pinot Noir** | **West Kelowna** *Red berry fruits, exotic spices, and a long finish*

Beer-Braised Short Ribs

When the weather turns and you're pining for good old-fashioned comfort food, braised short ribs hit all the notes. The meat needs to be seared in a really hot pan to get a good crust. And if your short ribs have a lot of fat on them, make the dish the day ahead and refrigerate overnight—you can easily skim off the layer of fat before reheating. Best of all, any good-quality local dark beer can be used for this recipe.

INGREDIENTS

2 lbs beef short ribs

⅓ cup all-purpose flour

1 tsp ground paprika

1 tsp coarsely ground black pepper, plus more for seasoning

¼ cup olive oil

2 medium carrots, cut into 2-inch pieces

2 stalks celery, cut into 2-inch pieces

½ medium leek, coarsely diced

1 large onion, halved and cut into ½-inch-thick slices

4 cloves garlic, sliced

1 cup beef stock

2 bay leaves

5 star anise pods

1 (11-fl oz) bottle dark beer such as Cannery Brewing's Naramata Nut Brown Ale

1½ cups canned diced tomatoes

6 sprigs thyme

2 sprigs rosemary

1 sprig sage

1 tsp salt

Mashed potatoes and grilled broccoli, to serve (optional)

Serves 4

FIRST Preheat oven to 300°F.

In a large bowl, combine the short ribs, flour, paprika, and pepper.

Heat a large skillet over medium-high heat, add the oil, and brown short ribs on all sides. Transfer the short ribs to a deep casserole dish. Add the carrots, celery, leeks, onion, and garlic to the same skillet and cook for 3 to 4 minutes, until slightly softened. Add a splash of the beef stock and scrape to help loosen any bits on the bottom of the pan. Transfer the mixture to the casserole dish, add the remaining ingredients, and spread evenly into the dish. Cover with foil and cook for 2 hours, until the ribs are fork tender. Remove the sprigs of herbs and discard. Season with salt and pepper to taste.

TO SERVE Divide the short ribs between 4 individual plates. Serve with mashed potatoes and grilled broccoli or your favourite side dishes.

+ **Sandhill Wines**   2012 Small Lots Barbera   **Kelowna**
Canada's only Barbera—cherry, berry, and plum with earthy notes

Beef Tenderloin and Smoked Salmon Roll with Crab Macaroni

While working at the Four Seasons Toronto Inn on the Park, a sous chef and I came up with this roll together. I questioned whether it would work since, well, it's a weird combination, but the results are delicious. It's also a decadent dish when you're having company, especially when it's served up with crab macaroni.

INGREDIENTS

1 (1½-lb) beef tenderloin, butterflied (ask your butcher)

10 to 12 slices smoked salmon

Sea salt and black pepper

2 Tbsp grapeseed oil

2 Tbsp capers

Green salad or steamed green vegetables, to serve

CRAB MACARONI

3 cups dried macaroni

2 Tbsp unsalted butter

2 large shallots, chopped

6 Tbsp white wine

2 cups whipping (35%) cream

2 sprigs tarragon

3 Tbsp finely grated horseradish

Sea salt and coarsely ground black pepper

6 oz crabmeat

Serves 4

FIRST Cover the beef evenly with the smoked salmon slices and roll into a tight long roll. Tie the beef roll with kitchen twine to keep it closed and season the roll with salt and pepper.

Preheat oven to 400°F. Heat a medium cast-iron or ovenproof skillet on medium-high heat, add a small amount of oil, and sear the beef roll for 2 to 3 minutes on each side until browned. Put the pan into the oven and roast for 25 to 30 minutes, for medium rare. Remove from oven and rest for 10 minutes.

CRAB MACARONI Bring a large saucepan of salted water to a boil over high heat, add the macaroni, and cook according to manufacturer's instructions. Drain and set aside.

Heat a pot on medium heat, add the butter and shallots, and cook for 1 to 2 minutes, until softened. Add the wine and cook for 3 to 4 minutes, until reduced by a third. Add the whipping cream, tarragon, and horseradish and cook for 10 minutes, stirring occasionally, until the sauce has thickened and reduced slightly. Transfer the sauce to a blender and blend until smooth. Season with salt and pepper. Combine the macaroni and sauce in a saucepan and heat over medium-low heat, until warmed through. Stir in the crabmeat.

TO SERVE Divide the macaroni onto 4 serving plates. Slice the beef and salmon roll and top the macaroni with slices. Garnish with capers, and serve with green salad or steamed green vegetables.

✦ CedarCreek Estate Winery | 2013 Meritage | Kelowna

A blend of Malbec, Cabernet Sauvignon, Merlot, and Cabernet Franc

Cocoa-Braised Oxtail with Mashed Potato and Celery Root

Down the street from my house is an old-school grocer who's been living the "nose to tail" movement since before it became trendy. Of course, he always has oxtail. This hearty, dark, cold-winter-night kind of meal makes for proper comfort food. (I often prepare the oxtails in advance and reheat them, which allows the flavours to really come together.) Get out the red wine.

2½ lbs oxtail, cut into 2- to 3-inch lengths

Sea salt and coarsely ground black pepper

¼ tsp ground smoked paprika

¼ cup grapeseed oil

1 large onion, finely chopped

2 stalks celery, finely chopped

2 large carrots, finely chopped

8 cloves garlic, finely chopped

½ cup red wine

2 cups beef broth

¼ cup red wine vinegar

¼ cup cocoa powder

ROASTED PARSNIPS (OPTIONAL)

4 medium parsnips, quartered lengthwise

2 Tbsp oil

Sea salt and pepper

Maple syrup, to drizzle

Serves 4

ROASTED PARSNIPS Put the parsnips, if making, on a baking sheet, drizzle over the olive oil, and season with salt and pepper. Mix well and set aside.

OXTAIL Preheat oven to 300°F.

Season the oxtails with salt, pepper, and paprika. Heat a large skillet over medium-high heat, add the oil, and then put in the oxtails. Sear for 8 to 10 minutes, until browned on all sides. Transfer to a deep casserole dish.

Return the pan to the stove, add the onions, celery, carrots, and garlic, and cook for 3 to 4 minutes, until softened. Pour in the red wine and cook for 1 minute, scraping the bottom of the pan to loosen any bits. Add the remaining ingredients and stir to incorporate.

Pour the mixture over the oxtails (leave some vegetables on top so it adds flavour), cover, put in the oven, and cook for 2¼ hours. Put the pan of parsnips in the oven, if making, and cook for another 45 minutes, until the parsnips are just cooked through and the oxtails are fork tender. Season the parsnips with salt and pepper and drizzle with maple syrup. *Continued overleaf*

MASHED POTATO AND CELERY ROOT

3 to 4 medium potatoes, chopped (about 2 cups)

1 cup chopped celery root

¼ cup extra-virgin olive oil

Sea salt and coarsely ground black pepper

CHEESE CRUNCH

¼ cup shredded Cheddar cheese

¼ cup shredded Parmigiano-Reggiano

¼ cup panko breadcrumbs

1 Tbsp chopped parsley

MASHED POTATO AND CELERY ROOT While the oxtails are braising, bring a pot of salted water to a boil, add the potatoes and celery root, and simmer for 15 to 20 minutes, until tender. Drain, transfer to a bowl, and mash. Add the oil and season with salt and pepper to taste.

CHEESE CRUNCH Line a baking sheet with parchment paper. In a small bowl, combine all the ingredients, mix well, and pour onto the prepared baking sheet. Spread out into a thin layer, add the sheet to the oven, and bake for 15 to 20 minutes. Set aside to cool, and then break into small pieces.

TO SERVE Divide the mash between 4 plates, top each serving with a few oxtails, and ladle over the chunky sauce. Sprinkle the cheese crunch overtop. Serve with the parsnips, if desired.

Bison Pot Roast with Smoked Paprika Butter and Crispy Kale

When I was growing up, Sunday pot roast was a tradition. Here, we take it up a notch with the bison, a hint of orange zest, and a splash of bourbon. Bison is lower in calories, fat, and cholesterol than beef, and it contains essential fatty acids, so you can feel virtuous cooking this one. Because the meat is lean, cook it low and slow to keep it tender.

INGREDIENTS

1 (2-lb) bison or beef chuck roast

Sea salt and coarsely ground black pepper

2 Tbsp grapeseed oil

1 large onion, cut into wedges

3 large carrots, cut into 1-inch pieces

3 stalks celery, cut into 2-inch lengths

2 oranges, cut into quarters

1½ cups beef broth

Baked buttermilk biscuits, to serve (optional)

SMOKED PAPRIKA BUTTER

1 cup (2 sticks) unsalted butter, room temperature

2 medium shallots, finely chopped

Finely grated zest of 1 orange

2 Tbsp Dijon mustard

1 tsp ground smoked paprika

Sea salt and coarsely ground black pepper

CRISPY KALE

1 bunch kale

1½ Tbsp soy sauce

1 tsp sesame oil

Serves 4

SMOKED PAPRIKA BUTTER Combine all the ingredients in a bowl and mix well. Cover and refrigerate until ready to use.

CRISPY KALE Line a baking sheet with parchment paper. Put the kale in a bowl, add the soy sauce and oil, and toss. Spread mixture onto the prepared baking sheet. Set aside.

BISON POT ROAST Preheat oven to 325°F.

Season the roast with salt and pepper. Heat a large cast-iron or ovenproof skillet over medium-high heat, add the bison, and sear for 2 to 3 minutes, until browned. Turn and sear for another 2 to 3 minutes, and repeat until all sides are browned. Transfer to a casserole dish, add the remaining ingredients, and cook for 2 hours. Add the kale pan to the oven and cook for another 25 minutes.

Remove both the bison and the kale from the oven and rest for 15 minutes.

TO SERVE Slice the pot roast into thick slices and put on 4 plates. Spoon over vegetables and braising liquid, top with a generous spoon of smoked paprika butter, and serve with crispy kale. Serve with buttermilk biscuits, if using.

The "Dog"

This recipe was inspired by a street vendor in Strasbourg, France, who was serving lamb merguez on a crusty bun with hot mustard, celery root slaw, and French fries piled on top. It was so delicious I can remember it to this day. This used to be on our menu at RauDZ. I even had custom hot dog plates made just for it. I think I'll have to bring it back again.

INGREDIENTS

4 skinny lamb merguez sausages

2 large hot dog or hoagie-style buns (see Note)

Hot mustard

French Fries (page 93), to serve

RJB Blackberry Ketchup (page 67), to serve (optional)

CELERY ROOT SLAW

½ cup shredded celery root

2 green onions, sliced

1 dill pickle, cut into thin strips

½ cup Mayonnaise (page 107)

3 dashes Worcestershire sauce

Sea salt and coarsely ground black pepper

NOTE The bun should be large enough to hold everything, with the French fries on top.

Makes 2

CELERY ROOT SLAW In a bowl, combine all the ingredients, toss, and season to taste with salt and pepper.

TO ASSEMBLE Preheat oven to 300°F.

Preheat a grill over medium heat. (Alternatively, heat a skillet over low to medium-low heat.) Add the sausages and grill (or pan-fry) for 5 to 7 minutes, until just cooked through.

Toast buns in the oven for 2 to 3 minutes, until the outsides are crisp. Spread mustard inside the buns, place 2 sausages in each, and top with celery root slaw and French fries.

TO SERVE Place the hot dogs on 2 individual plates and serve with RJB Blackberry Ketchup, if using.

+ Bad Tattoo Brewing | **Los Muertos Cerveza Negra** | **Penticton**
A dark lager, reminiscent of a light German bock

Pork Roast with Apples and Potatoes

Tradition doesn't taste any better than pork with apples and potatoes, served family style. Brining is key for tender, moist pork or chicken: it breaks down the tissues and introduces moisture to the meat. At the restaurant, we routinely brine our meats for 18 to 24 hours. It is a great trick for the home cook.

INGREDIENTS

1 (2-lb) pork loin roast

6 slices bacon

BRINE

2 cups water

2 cups apple juice

¼ cup apple cider vinegar

¼ cup sugar

1 medium onion, chopped

1 stalk celery, chopped

3 cloves garlic, chopped

3 bay leaves

6 whole cloves

3 Tbsp kosher salt

1 tsp black peppercorns

APPLES AND POTATOES

4 to 6 large red potatoes, unpeeled, cut into large wedges

2 large apples, cored and cut into wedges

1 Tbsp chopped rosemary

Sea salt and black pepper

¼ cup olive oil

CABBAGE SLAW

1½ cups finely shredded green cabbage

1½ cups finely shredded Savoy cabbage

4 green onions, chopped

1 Tbsp yellow or black mustard seeds

3 Tbsp apple cider vinegar

2 Tbsp honey

Serves 4

BRINE Combine all ingredients in a pot and simmer for 5 to 10 minutes over medium heat. Transfer to a large bowl and set aside to cool entirely. Carefully lower the pork roast into the brine, ensuring that it's completely submerged. Refrigerate, covered, for 18 to 24 hours.

APPLES AND POTATOES Combine all the ingredients in a large bowl and toss to mix. Set aside.

PORK ROAST Preheat oven to 350°F. Remove the pork from the brine and rinse under cold water. Put on a cutting board, pat-dry with paper towels, and lay the bacon slices on top. Wrap kitchen twine lightly around the roast and tie to hold the bacon in place. Put the loin in a large roasting pan and roast for 25 minutes.

Add the apples and potatoes to the roasting pan and cook for another 50 to 75 minutes, until tender and cooked through.

Remove from the oven and set aside to rest for 10 minutes.

CABBAGE SLAW In a large bowl, combine all the ingredients together and mix well. Chill until needed.

TO SERVE Transfer the apples and potatoes to a large serving plate. Slice the pork loin and arrange on a platter. Serve the cabbage slaw on the side.

✛ Tree Brewing | Dukes Dry Apple Cider | Kelowna
Made with 100 percent Kelowna apples, crisp and dry

Wild Boar Meatball with Vegetable Tomato Ragout

These are served as one big meatball per portion, not the usual Ping Pong–size meatballs. The making of a good meatball is a labour of love, so take the time to do it right. We get our wild boar locally, but you can always use pork instead.

INGREDIENTS

5 slices white bread, crusts removed, cut into ½-inch cubes

½ cup milk

1½ lbs ground wild boar or high-quality ground pork

½ cup finely chopped aged Swiss-style cheese, such as Kootenay Alpindon

½ cup shredded Parmigiano-Reggiano

¼ cup chopped parsley

1 Tbsp Worcestershire sauce

1 tsp sea salt

1 tsp black pepper

½ tsp ground cinnamon

1 Tbsp grapeseed oil, for frying

Warm crusty bread, to serve

VEGETABLE TOMATO RAGOUT

¼ cup olive oil

1 small onion, sliced

½ cup chopped zucchini

1 cup chopped eggplant

1 medium red bell pepper, seeded and finely chopped

1 medium Belgian endive, leaves separated and left whole

1 cup cherry tomatoes, halved

3 Tbsp balsamic vinegar

¼ cup torn basil leaves

Sea salt and coarsely ground black pepper

NOTE Meatballs can be chilled, sliced, and used to make excellent sandwiches.

Serves 4 to 6

FIRST Put the bread cubes in a large bowl, pour in the milk, and soak for 3 to 4 minutes until softened. Add the ground boar (or pork) through cinnamon and use your hands to mix thoroughly. Divide equally into 4 to 6 large meatballs.

In a large skillet over medium heat, heat the oil, add the meatballs, turning to brown slightly, and pan-fry for 35 to 40 minutes, until cooked through. A lid can be used to cover the pan. (Alternatively, bake for 45 minutes in a 375°F oven.) Transfer the meatballs to an ovenproof dish (reserving the skillet for the ragout) and keep warm in the oven at 175°F.

VEGETABLE TOMATO RAGOUT In a skillet over medium-high heat (the same skillet the meatballs were cooked in, if possible), heat the oil. Add the onions, zucchini, and eggplant and sauté for 4 to 6 minutes, until slightly cooked. Add the bell peppers and cook for another 1 to 2 minutes, until the vegetables have softened. Stir in the remaining ingredients and cook for 3 minutes, until warmed through. Season to taste with salt and pepper.

TO SERVE Spoon the ragout onto a platter and place the meatballs on top. Serve with warm crusty bread.

Lamb T-Bones with Braised Cipollini, Mint Chutney, and Vegetable Chips

Lamb T-bones, often sold as loin chops, are grilled to perfection and served with sweet cipollini onions and super-easy-to-make mint chutney, which is a play on the traditional English mint-and-lamb pairing. If you're pressed for time, use high-quality, store-bought vegetable chips.

INGREDIENTS

2 cloves garlic, chopped

1 medium shallot, chopped

1 Tbsp chopped mint

1 Tbsp white wine vinegar

1 Tbsp olive oil

Sea salt and black pepper

8 lamb T-bones, about 1 inch thick

MINT CHUTNEY

1 Tbsp finely chopped ginger

1 cup mint leaves

½ cup unsweetened shredded coconut

1 to 2 pinches chili flakes

¼ cup plain yogurt

Juice of 1 large lime

Sea salt and coarsely ground black pepper

VEGETABLE CHIPS

2 cups grapeseed oil, for deep-frying

1 medium carrot

1 medium turnip

1 medium beet

Sea salt

BRAISED CIPOLLINI

4 Tbsp unsalted butter

12 cipollini onions, peeled and kept whole

Small bunch thyme

⅓ cup chicken stock

Serves 4

FIRST Combine the garlic, shallots, mint, vinegar, and olive oil, and season with salt and pepper. Rub the mixture over the lamb and set aside for 15 to 30 minutes to marinate.

MINT CHUTNEY Combine the ingredients in a food processor and blend until smooth. Season to taste with salt and pepper, transfer to a bowl, and refrigerate until needed.

VEGETABLE CHIPS Heat the oil in a heavy-bottomed saucepan, until it reaches a temperature of 325°F. Using a mandoline, thinly slice the vegetables. Gently lower the carrots and turnips into the hot oil, in batches, and deep-fry for 2 to 5 minutes, until light and crispy. Transfer to a plate lined with paper towels. Repeat with the beets. Season with salt and set aside.

BRAISED CIPOLLINI Heat a small skillet over medium heat, melt the butter, and add the onions. Cook for 3 to 5 minutes, until lightly browned. Add the thyme and stock, cover, and cook for another 10 to 15 minutes, until tender. Keep warm over low heat until needed.

TO ASSEMBLE Preheat BBQ to medium-high. Using paper towels, lightly pat the lamb chops dry, removing excess marinade. Put the lamb chops on the grill and sear for 4 to 6 minutes, until slightly charred. Flip over and cook for another 3 to 5 minutes, depending on the thickness, for medium. Transfer the lamb chops to a platter and serve with the braised onions, chutney, and vegetable chips.

Lamb Osso Buco with Mashed Red Jacket Potatoes

Osso buco is traditionally prepared with veal shanks, but my version has fork-tender lamb shanks braised in aromatic goodness. It preserves the Mediterranean profile with the rosemary and thyme, and the white wine braise balances out the richness of the meat.

INGREDIENTS

3 Tbsp grapeseed oil

4 lamb shanks

Sea salt and coarsely ground black pepper

1 Tbsp ground cumin

3 medium leeks, sliced

4 Tbsp Dijon mustard

2 sprigs rosemary

1 Tbsp chopped thyme leaves

3 sprigs mint

½ cup white wine

1½ cups chicken stock

Salad or steamed vegetables, to serve

RED JACKET POTATOES

4 to 6 medium red potatoes, unpeeled, chopped

1 Tbsp unsalted butter

3 Tbsp sour cream

1 large shallot, finely chopped

2 Tbsp finely chopped chives, plus extra for garnish

Serves 4

FIRST Preheat oven to 325°F.

Heat a large skillet over medium-high heat and add the oil to the pan. Season the lamb shanks with salt, pepper, and cumin, put in the pan, and sear for 2 to 3 minutes on each side, until browned. Transfer to a deep casserole dish.

Add the remaining ingredients to the pan and cook for 2 to 3 minutes, until fragrant. Pour the mixture over the lamb shanks, cover with a lid or foil, and cook for 1 hour. Reduce the heat to 300°F and cook for another hour, until the lamb is fork tender. Remove and keep hot.

RED JACKET POTATOES Bring a pot of salted water to a boil and add the potatoes. Reduce heat to medium and simmer for 30 to 35 minutes, until cooked through. Drain, transfer to a large bowl, and mash.

Add the remaining ingredients to the bowl and stir. Cover and keep warm until needed.

TO SERVE Place the shanks on 4 plates and pour over some of the braising liquid. Serve with the mashed potatoes and a salad or steamed vegetables.

+ **Burrowing Owl Estate Winery**   **2012 Cabernet Sauvignon**   **Oliver**
Blackberry, cassis, and plum with dried herbs, full bodied with great acidity

Grilled Venison Chops with Grains and Pumpkin Seed Mustard

With multi-grains, dried blueberries, and red kuri squash, this hearty venison dish is an ode to fall. Because venison is a very lean meat, be extremely careful not to overcook. We serve it medium rare at the restaurant.

INGREDIENTS

2 (8-oz) venison chops
¼ tsp sea salt
¼ tsp black pepper
1 Tbsp grapeseed oil, for pan-frying

GRAINS

1 Tbsp unsalted butter
1 small onion, finely chopped
¼ cup farro
¼ cup wild rice
¼ cup pearl barley
2 Tbsp chopped mixed herbs
¼ cup dried blueberries
2 cups chicken stock
Sea salt and black pepper

RED KURI SQUASH

½ medium red kuri squash, seeds and stringy bits removed, cut into wedges
3 Tbsp unsalted butter, melted
1 tsp ground nutmeg
Sea salt and black pepper

PUMPKIN SEED MUSTARD

¼ cup Dijon mustard
3 Tbsp shelled pumpkin seeds, crushed
Finely grated zest of ¼ orange
Pinch of allspice

Serves 2

GRAINS In a pot over medium heat, melt the butter and add the onions. Sauté for 2 to 3 minutes and then add the remaining ingredients. Stir and bring to a soft boil. Reduce the heat to low, cover, and simmer for 45 minutes, or until the grains are tender. Season with salt and pepper.

RED KURI SQUASH Preheat oven to 350°F. Put the squash wedges in a bowl, add the melted butter, and sprinkle over the nutmeg. Toss, transfer to a baking sheet, and roast for 30 to 40 minutes, until tender. Season with salt and pepper.

PUMPKIN SEED MUSTARD Combine the ingredients in a small bowl and mix.

VENISON CHOPS Preheat BBQ to medium-high heat. Season chops with salt and pepper, add to the BBQ, and grill for 5 to 7 minutes. Flip and grill for another 3 to 5 minutes, depending on the thickness of the chops, until just cooked through. (Alternatively, preheat a large skillet on medium-high heat, add the oil, add the chops, and sear for 5 to 7 minutes. Flip and sear for another 3 to 5 minutes.) Transfer to a plate and set aside to rest.

TO SERVE Spoon grains onto 2 plates. Place squash and venison chops on top. Spoon pumpkin seed mustard onto the chops and serve.

✚ C.C. Jentsch Cellars | 2013 Syrah | Oliver

A classic Syrah, a grape varietal that is considered by many to be a perfect pair with grilled venison!

Strawberry Cream Cheese Mousse

Not your average mousse. Whenever I crave something sweet, this cloud of goodness is my personal favourite. It's a variation on strawberries and cream: bursts of fruit balanced with cold creaminess and offset by tangy cream cheese and vibrant citrus zests.

INGREDIENTS

1 cup (8-oz) cream cheese, room temperature

⅓ cup icing sugar, sifted

Juice and finely grated zest of 1 orange

Finely grated zest of 1 lime

Finely grated zest of 1 lemon

1 tsp vanilla extract

13 to 15 fresh strawberries, lightly mashed (see Note)

1½ cups whipping (35%) cream

3 egg whites

2½ Tbsp granulated sugar

Sliced strawberries, for garnish (optional)

NOTE Frozen strawberries can also be used in a pinch—simply thaw and drain the juices before adding them to the recipe.

Serves 4

FIRST Using a stand mixer with the paddle attachment, combine the cream cheese, icing sugar, zests, vanilla extract, and orange juice and mix well, scraping down the sides of the bowl. Add the strawberries and mix until incorporated. Remove and set aside.

Put the whipping cream in a clean mixing bowl and, using the whisk attachment, whip until firm peaks form. (Alternatively, whisk by hand.) Transfer to another dish and set aside.

Clean out the mixing bowl thoroughly, add the egg whites, and whip until medium peaks form. Slowly add the sugar.

Fold the whipped cream into the strawberry-cream cheese mixture and then fold the whipped egg whites into the mixture. Pour into a large serving bowl or individual bowls and refrigerate for 3 to 4 hours, until set.

TO SERVE Serve chilled in individual bowls or family style, encouraging everyone to help themselves. Garnish with sliced strawberries, if using.

Double Chocolate Mashed Potato Brioche

This dish was partly inspired by a warm chocolate dessert that my grandmother would make. The other inspiration came from the mashed potato craze of the 1990s. It's one of those can't-stop-eating-this desserts, and a huge hit at the restaurant. We serve it with warm chocolate sauce, raspberry compote, and raspberry sorbet.

INGREDIENTS

5 oz dark chocolate, broken into pieces

1 Tbsp instant coffee

3 Tbsp amaretto

½ cup (1 stick) unsalted butter, in chunks

4 eggs, separated

½ cup granulated sugar

1 cup mashed potatoes (I prefer russet)

½ cup ground almonds

Pinch of salt

½ cup milk chocolate chips

Warm chocolate sauce, to serve

Raspberry compote, to serve

Raspberry sorbet, to serve

Makes 8

FIRST Set a bowl over a pot of simmering water or a double boiler, add the broken chocolate, coffee, amaretto, and butter, and stir for 3 to 4 minutes, or until chocolate has melted. Set aside.

In a separate bowl, beat the egg yolks and sugar until thick and creamy. Add the chocolate mixture to the bowl and stir to mix. Add the mashed potatoes and ground almonds and mix until thoroughly combined.

In another bowl, beat the egg whites until stiff and fold into the chocolate mixture. Add the salt and gently fold in the chocolate chips.

Preheat oven to 350°F, spoon the mixture into 8 small brioche moulds (or use a muffin pan), three-quarters full, and bake for 30 minutes, until risen. Set aside to cool for 15 minutes, then remove from the moulds.

TO SERVE Serve the brioches on individual plates with warm chocolate sauce, raspberry compote, and raspberry sorbet.

Apricot Curd Tart

My chef de cuisine Robyn Sigurdson, who has worked with us since Fresco, came up with this simple and yummy tart, showing off the tasty union that is apricot and thyme.

APRICOT CURD FILLING

2 tsp gelatin powder

2 cups apricot purée (divided)

1 tsp thyme leaves

6 egg yolks

½ cup granulated sugar

ALMOND PASTRY

½ cup almonds

2 cups all-purpose flour, plus extra for dusting

1 cup (2 sticks) unsalted butter, room temperature

¾ cup brown sugar

1 egg

Makes 8 (4-inch) tarts

APRICOT CURD FILLING Combine gelatin powder with 1 cup of apricot purée. Set aside for 2 minutes to let the gelatin bloom.

In a heatproof bowl, combine the remaining 1 cup purée, thyme leaves, egg yolks, and sugar and place over a pot of simmering water. Stir continuously until it starts to thicken. Add the gelatin mixture and stir until the gelatin has dissolved and the mixture is thick enough to coat the back of a spoon. Pour into a shallow dish and place a piece of plastic wrap directly over the curd. (This will help avoid a skin forming on top.) Cool in the fridge for at least 2 hours.

ALMOND PASTRY In a food processor, process the nuts until fine. Add the flour and process until mixed.

Using a stand mixer, cream together the butter and brown sugar. Add the egg and mix until combined. Add the flour mixture and mix until it just comes together. (Do not overmix.)

Remove the dough from the bowl, form into a rectangle, and wrap tightly with plastic wrap. Refrigerate for 1 hour, until firm.

Preheat oven to 350°F. Grease 8 (4-inch) tart pans and set aside.

Unwrap the dough, place on a floured surface, and roll out to a ¼-inch thickness. *Continued overleaf*

MERINGUE
1 cup granulated sugar
¼ cup water
4 egg whites

Cut out 8 circles 1 inch larger than the tart pans and mould the shells into the pans. Trim the edges, if required, and refrigerate for 30 minutes, until firm.

Prick the shells all over with a fork, line them with parchment paper, and fill with dried beans or pie weights. (This prevents the shells from blistering and shrinking.) Bake for 5 minutes, remove the beans (or weights) and parchment paper, and bake for another 10 minutes, until golden. Set aside to cool.

MERINGUE In a small pot over high heat, combine the sugar and water and heat until it reaches a temperature of 230°F.

Put the egg whites in a large bowl and whisk to stiff peaks. Continuing to whisk, pour in the syrup and whip until completely cool. Set aside.

TO ASSEMBLE Remove curd from the fridge and stir. Divide the mixture evenly among the tart shells, and use a piping bag or spatula to top with the meringue.

TO SERVE Using a kitchen torch, brulée the top of the meringue on each tart until light brown. Serve.

Caramel Crunch

Think of a Coffee Crisp chocolate bar. Here, we've deconstructed it with chocolate *crémeux* (French for "creamy," it's a dense, soft, classic pudding) and sponge toffee. The trickiest part is the toffee candy, because you have to work quickly. The best part is that it is sinfully delicious. If you don't have an ice-cream maker, buy a high-quality caramel ice cream and garnish with salt.

CHOCOLATE CRÉMEUX

5 egg yolks

¼ cup granulated sugar

1 cup milk

2 Tbsp chilled unsalted butter, cut into ½-inch cubes

½ cup finely chopped milk chocolate

½ cup finely chopped dark chocolate

Coarse sea salt, to serve (optional)

TOFFEE

Cooking spray

½ cup granulated sugar

½ cup corn syrup

¾ tsp white vinegar

1½ tsp baking soda

Serves 8

CHOCOLATE CRÉMEUX Using a stand mixer, combine the egg yolks and sugar and, using the whisk attachment, whisk for 5 minutes, or until doubled in volume. Add milk and mix well.

Pour the milk mixture into a heatproof bowl and place on top of a pot of simmering water. Stir continuously (to prevent the eggs from overcooking) and cook for 4 to 6 minutes, until it's thick enough to coat the back of a wooden spoon.

In a large bowl, combine butter and all the chocolate and set aside. Pour the milk mixture into the bowl and whisk until combined and chocolate has completely melted. Pour into a container and refrigerate for at least 1 hour until set. (Makes 2 cups.)

TOFFEE Line a metal loaf pan or deep casserole dish with parchment paper and spray the paper with cooking spray.

In a medium pot over high heat, combine the sugar, corn syrup, and vinegar and heat until it reaches a temperature of 300°F. (It's very important to work quickly at this point.)

Remove the pan from heat, quickly add the baking soda, and vigorously whisk until well mixed. Pour the mixture into the prepared pan or dish and set aside for 30 to 45 minutes. (Do not move or touch the toffee as it expands.)

Remove toffee and break into small pieces. Store in an airtight container until needed. (Makes 1½ cups.) *Continued overleaf*

SALTED CARAMEL ICE CREAM

¾ cup granulated sugar

¼ cup water

2 ¼ cups whipping (35%) cream

¾ cup milk

3 eggs

¼ tsp salt

SALTED CARAMEL ICE CREAM Combine the sugar and water in a deep pot and stir. Cook, untouched, over high heat for 7 to 10 minutes, until a dark caramel colour. Remove the pot from the heat, add the cream, and quickly whisk until combined. (Don't worry if it comes to a rapid boil, this is normal.)

Combine milk and eggs in a large bowl and mix well. Pour a little of the hot mixture into the bowl and whisk. Whisking continuously, slowly pour the remaining hot mixture into the bowl. Add the salt and stir, then strain and cool. Refrigerate for at least 3 hours.

Pour the mixture into an ice-cream machine and churn for 20 to 30 minutes (or follow manufacturer's instructions). (Makes 4 cups.)

TO SERVE Spoon the chocolate crémeux into individual bowls or glasses, top with a scoop of salted caramel ice cream, and garnish with the toffee. Finish each bowl with a pinch of coarse sea salt, if desired. Serve immediately.

TWILIGHT

My twilight time philosophy is to pack the maximum amount of flavour into that small bite. It comes together with the perfectly balanced sip.

AFTER ALL, cocktail hour is the celebratory hour, when the sun has set and work is done and people want to put their stresses aside. These recipes will be just the trick to get them on their way.

If you were to make them all, the cocktails and tapas items in this chapter would add up to a killer cocktail party. Many of the tapas can be prepared ahead of time, and they also work terrifically as rustic, fuss-free pre-dinner appetizers. Serve these tapas on your nicest wood carving boards or big ceramic plates. Get out the tumblers, vintage glassware, and that ceramic jug from that trip to Spain. Dim the lights or get out the patio lanterns to create the same warm, intimate atmosphere that we've created at micro bar • bites—my cozy little establishment up the street from RauDZ.

Farm-to-glass beverages have now become a major trend in the restaurant scene, which is great, because it's meant the arrival of a slew of local breweries and distilleries. At micro, our philosophy behind the bar is the exact same as in the kitchen at RauDZ: farm fresh, as local as possible, and using the best-quality ingredients.

We do seasonal cocktail menus the same way we do seasonal food menus. In winter, we make use of all the fruits and vegetables that we froze and preserved at peak season. But if you can't find a good-quality ingredient, use your creativity and swap it out for another. Maybe use plums instead of peaches. And with the help of a little juice or fizzy water, all of these cocktails can be made without alcohol.

When looking for the right drink pairings for a meal at home, take a look around your own region and visit wineries if there are any nearby. Otherwise, see if you can find a local distillery that's making an interesting herbal gin, high-quality vodka, or whisky. Distilleries and microbreweries are everywhere these days,

and they've become one of the favourite new industries. If you don't have nearby access, go online.

And to make the best cocktail you will need some equipment, including a Boston shaker, a Hawthorne strainer, a muddler, a long mixing spoon, and a blender. These items aren't expensive, and they'll make the job so much easier.

Naturally, you'll want to pair great finger foods with great cocktails. I chose a few of our easiest and favourite tapas dishes. In the **Stuffed Calamari** recipe **[page 228]**, the small squid don't require cleaning like big squid do, and you can either pan-fry or barbecue them. The **Duck Fat Popcorn [page 225]** is salty, fatty decadence—there was no way we could leave our popcorn out of this book. A staple at micro, it's so simple and addictive, you'll wonder how you could have lived without it.

Amante Picante

This is the creation of our legendary former bar manager, Gerry Jobe, who really drove the entire cocktail program. It's savoury meets sweet, with a tickle of TABASCO, and our customers love it.

4 cucumber slices

8 sprigs cilantro

1 fl oz reposado tequila

1 fl oz Triple Sec

2 fl oz fresh lime juice

½ Tbsp honey (I prefer Brainy Bee)

4 dashes TABASCO Green Jalapeño Pepper Sauce

Salted cucumber slice or lime wedge, for garnish

Serves 1

FIRST Muddle cucumber slices and cilantro in a shaker. Add the remaining ingredients and some ice. Shake for 1 minute and double-strain into a glass.

TO SERVE Garnish with a salted cucumber slice or a lime wedge, if desired, and serve.

Ambrosia Salad

Bartender Danielle Jeckel came up with this ode to the 1970s classic the ambrosia salad, and it really does taste just like it. It's definitely got that warm southern feel to it, spicy and complex, and it's not as sweet as it sounds.

INGREDIENTS

1 slice lemon

3 raspberries

2 peach slices

2 fl oz Bulleit Bourbon

¼ fl oz Okanagan Spirits Raspberry Liqueur

½ fl oz Toasted Marshmallow Syrup (recipe here)

1 dash Bittered Sling Clingstone Peach Bitters

¼ fl oz Amontillado sherry

Mint leaves, for garnish

TOASTED MARSHMALLOW SYRUP

1 cup water

1 cup granulated sugar

8 large marshmallows

1 tsp vanilla extract

Serves 1

TOASTED MARSHMALLOW SYRUP Bring water and sugar to a boil in a small pot, then turn off the heat.

Using a BBQ lighter or kitchen torch, lightly toast the marshmallows. Stir them into the hot syrup and incorporate. Add the vanilla, stir, and let stand for at least 1 hour.

Strain syrup into a bowl and refrigerate until use. It can be kept for 2 to 3 weeks. (Makes 1 cup.)

NEXT In a Boston shaker, muddle the lemon slice, raspberries, and peach slices. Add the bourbon, raspberry liqueur, marshmallow syrup, and bitters, shake for a minute, and double-strain into a large glass.

TO SERVE Fill the glass with cracked or crushed ice, top with the sherry, and garnish with mint.

Bacon-Wrapped Plums

This is our version of angels on horseback (a savoury canapé of bacon-wrapped oysters), but in my opinion, tastier. I buy the plums from farmers who have heirloom plum trees. If you can't find fresh plums, use dried prune plums, and rehydrate them a little bit. We serve this in the restaurant on our fall/winter menu.

16 fresh or dried Italian prune plums, pitted

8 slices bacon, halved lengthwise

BLUE CHEESE MOUSSE

¼ cup + ⅓ cup whipping (35%) cream (divided)

1 tsp gelatin powder

¼ cup blue cheese

PORT WINE SYRUP

¼ cup port wine

2 Tbsp honey

2 whole cloves

6 black peppercorns

Makes 16

FIRST If using fresh plums, preheat oven to 275°F and dry them for about 1 hour on a baking sheet. If using dried plums, put them in a small bowl, cover with water, and set aside for 10 to 15 minutes, until reconstituted.

BLUE CHEESE MOUSSE In a small saucepan, combine ¼ cup whipping cream and the gelatin and set aside for 5 minutes to bloom. Add the blue cheese and cook on low heat, until the cheese has melted. Strain into a small bowl and refrigerate for 15 to 20 minutes, until just cooled. (The mixture must remain liquidy and not fully set.)

Meanwhile, whip the remaining ⅓ cup of whipping cream until medium peaks form. Fold in the blue cheese mixture, and transfer to a piping bag or airtight container until needed.

PORT WINE SYRUP Combine the ingredients in a small pot over medium heat and cook for 5 to 7 minutes, until syrupy. Set aside to cool, then chill.

TO ASSEMBLE Preheat oven to 400°F. Wrap a piece of bacon around a plum and place on a baking sheet. Repeat with the remainder and bake for 8 to 10 minutes, until the bacon is golden.

TO SERVE Transfer the plums to serving spoons, top with blue cheese mousse, and drizzle over the port wine syrup.

Autumn in the Valley

Bartender Trevor Seaby created this cocktail to capture the spirit of
the season while preparing a Thanksgiving dinner. This drink is a lot like
a whisky sour, but the warmth of the ginger speaks of fall and holidays.

INGREDIENTS
3 sage leaves
2 fl oz Dark Horse rye
1 fl oz Ginger Honey (recipe here)
½ fl oz fresh lemon juice
1 egg white (optional)

GINGER HONEY
½ cup water
Pinch of salt
2 Tbsp finely chopped ginger
Peel of 1 orange
½ cup honey (I prefer Arlo's honey)

Serves 1

GINGER HONEY In a small pot, bring water and salt to a boil.
Add the ginger and orange peel and simmer for 10 minutes.
Add the honey and stir until dissolved. Strain and chill.
(Ginger honey can be stored in the fridge for up to 2 weeks.)

NEXT Put the sage into a Boston shaker and stamp with a
muddler or the end of a wooden spoon. Add the remaining
ingredients and dry-shake (shaking the mixture first without
ice helps mix the egg). Add ice and shake again for a minute.

TO SERVE Strain through a fine strainer into a coupe glass and
serve straight up or on the rocks.

Duck Fat Popcorn

Popcorn with duck fat is incredibly addictive. This one comes right off our micro bar • bites menu, and our customers rave about it. Duck fat can be found at any good gourmet food store, or your local butcher or farmers' market. Or, next time you cook duck, save the fat. It's decadent and arguably healthy, too, since it contains more unsaturated fat than saturated. Regardless, this popcorn is a delicious treat.

INGREDIENTS

3 Tbsp vegetable oil

½ cup popcorn kernels

4 to 6 Tbsp duck fat, melted and warmed

1 to 2 Tbsp chopped rosemary leaves

Flaked sea salt (Maldon preferred) and coarsely ground black pepper

Serves 1 to 2

FIRST Heat the oil in a large heavy-bottomed saucepan over moderate heat, add the popcorn kernels, and cover. Cook for 3 to 5 minutes, shaking the pan frequently, until the kernels stop popping. Transfer to a large bowl.

TO SERVE Drizzle the popcorn with the warm duck fat and sprinkle over the rosemary. Season with salt and pepper to taste. Prepare for addiction.

✚ Tree Brewing | Kelowna Pilsner | Kelowna
Refreshing malt flavour, mild hop finish

Backyard Rhubarb Lemonade

Our former bar manager Gerry Jobe would eat rhubarb stalks dipped in sugar as a kid, and this is his nod to that childhood memory. Served in a Mason jar, this cocktail is a taste of summer.

INGREDIENTS

1 fl oz vodka (I prefer Okanagan Spirits)
1 fl oz Raspberry Purée (recipe here)
1 fl oz Rhubarb Purée (recipe here)
3 fl oz Lemon Syrup (page 231)
1 stalk sugar-dipped rhubarb, for garnish

RASPBERRY PURÉE
½ cup raspberries
1½ Tbsp granulated sugar

RHUBARB PURÉE
½ cup chopped rhubarb
2 Tbsp granulated sugar

Serves 1

RASPBERRY PURÉE Combine the ingredients in a blender and purée until smooth. Strain to remove seeds. Chill.

RHUBARB PURÉE Combine the rhubarb and sugar in a small pot and cook over medium heat for 10 minutes, until tender. Transfer to a blender and purée until smooth. Chill.

TO SERVE Fill a 2-cup (16-fl oz) Mason jar with ice. Pour vodka, raspberry, and rhubarb purée into the jar, top with Lemon Syrup, and stir well. Garnish with a sugar-dipped stalk of rhubarb and a straw.

Stuffed Calamari

This is a long-time signature dish of ours. We use small calamari tubes, so it's ideal finger food. The baby calamari tubes are tender and the sun-dried tomato, olive, and Parmesan stuffing gives them a bold flavour. Any memories of the tough deep-fried rings of calamari often found in restaurants will be banished forever.

INGREDIENTS

18 to 24 (⅝-inch) frozen calamari tubes (also known as baby calamari), thawed

STUFFING

5 cloves garlic, chopped

1 shallot, chopped

2 Tbsp grapeseed oil, plus extra for brushing

12 sun-dried black olives, pitted

3 canned or jarred anchovies

⅓ cup shredded Parmigiano-Reggiano

¼ cup panko or regular breadcrumbs

¼ cup sun-dried tomatoes, chopped

3 Tbsp extra-virgin olive oil

2 Tbsp chopped parsley

Coarsely ground black pepper

Makes 18 to 24 pieces

STUFFING Heat the oil in a small skillet over medium heat, add the garlic and shallots, and cook for 1 to 2 minutes, until just translucent. Set aside.

Put the garlic and shallots in a food processor, add the remaining ingredients, and blend until it comes together. (It will be coarse.)

CALAMARI Using a spoon and a kitchen funnel (inserted into the open ends of the calamari tubes), scoop the stuffing and fill each calamari three-quarters full. (The funnel makes stuffing them easier.)

Heat BBQ or stovetop grill to medium-high heat. Brush a bit of oil on the calamari tubes and grill for 3 to 5 minutes, until the calamari is cooked through and the stuffing is hot. (Do not overcook.)

TO SERVE Transfer the stuffed calamari to a serving platter and serve immediately.

Fresh Fruit Martini

This martini is best made with vodka, which works as a clean-tasting backdrop for the fruit. We always have three fresh fruit martinis on the menu each day, and the fruit purée depends entirely on what's in season. When fruits are out of season, we make use of our homemade preserves, such as strawberry, raspberry, or quince. It's a good reason to get in the habit of summer preserving.

INGREDIENTS

1 fl oz Okanagan Spirits Vodka

1 fl oz Triple Sec

2 fl oz Fruit Purée (recipe here)

2 fl oz Lemon Syrup (recipe here)

Edible flower or fresh fruit slice, for garnish

FRUIT PURÉE

1 cup fresh fruit, such as strawberries

2 Tbsp granulated sugar

LEMON SYRUP

¼ cup fresh lemon juice

3 Tbsp granulated sugar

Serves 1

FRUIT PURÉE Put the ingredients in a small saucepan and cook for 5 minutes over low heat. Transfer to a blender and purée until smooth. Strain through a fine-mesh strainer and chill.

LEMON SYRUP In a small bowl, combine the ingredients and stir until the sugar has dissolved.

NEXT Fill a Boston shaker half full of ice, add the martini ingredients, and shake vigorously for 1 minute.

TO SERVE Strain the mixture into a classic martini glass and garnish with an edible flower or slice of fruit.

Fresh Figs

Sure, dried figs are available year round, but there's something special about fresh figs. Split open to reveal their inner seeds, they are beautiful on the plate, rich in flavour, and not too sweet. This dish is a nod to the Mediterranean, a marriage of the sweet flavours of fig and honey and the creamy tang of feta.

INGREDIENTS

8 fresh figs, stem removed

2 Tbsp honey

1 to 2 pinches chili flakes

2 Tbsp crushed hazelnuts

1 to 2 oz feta cheese, crumbled

Makes 8

FIRST Make 2 cross cuts, top to bottom, through each fig, taking care not to cut through it entirely. Pull the 4 quarters of each one slightly apart to expose the insides. Place the figs on a serving plate.

TO SERVE Drizzle the figs with honey, and sprinkle with chili flakes, hazelnuts, and feta cheese, both inside and out. Serve.

Lavender Bee's Knees

This simple and delicious drink is the creation of our bartender Ben Hefford. Locally grown honey—with its many flavour nuances—is well worth sourcing. Honey and lemon are obvious friends, but the freshness of the lemon and the small amount of honey keep this cocktail from becoming something you'd stick a little paper umbrella into. It's a grown-up drink for gin lovers.

INGREDIENTS

2 fl oz Okanagan Spirits Gin
1 fl oz lavender honey
½ fl oz fresh lemon juice
3 dashes Bittered Sling Grapefruit & Hops Bitters
Thin lemon wheel, for garnish

Serves 1

FIRST Fill a Boston shaker with ice, add the ingredients, and shake vigorously for 1 minute.

TO SERVE Strain into a coupe glass and garnish with a thin lemon wheel.

Guanciale and Escalivada on Toast

I thank talented micro bar • bites chef Chris Braun for this delicious contribution. Guanciale is Italian cured pork jowl and in this dish, it is served with a savoury-sweet compote. You get the richness of the pork, the sweetness of honey and almond butter, and the charred goodness of the veggies, all on a toasted baguette.

INGREDIENTS

⅓ cup Almond Butter (recipe here)

1 long baguette, cut diagonally into 1-inch-thick slices, toasted (12 pieces)

1½ cups Escalivada (recipe here)

12 thin slices guanciale, prosciutto, or any cured-style bacon

Chopped mixed herbs, to garnish (optional)

ESCALIVADA

½ red bell pepper, seeded and sliced into ¼-inch strips

½ yellow bell pepper, seeded and sliced into ¼-inch strips

½ cup chopped eggplant (½-inch cubes)

½ medium red onion, cut into ½-inch slices

6 cloves garlic, finely chopped

1 Tbsp chopped dill

1 Tbsp chopped flat-leaf parsley

¼ cup olive oil

¼ cup white vinegar

2 Tbsp honey

Juice of 1 lemon

ALMOND BUTTER

⅓ cup blanched whole almonds

3 Tbsp olive oil, plus extra if needed

½ tsp ground cinnamon

½ tsp caraway seeds

Salt and pepper

Makes 12

ESCALIVADA In a large bowl, combine the peppers, eggplant, onions, garlic, and herbs and toss.

In a small bowl, combine the oil, vinegar, honey, and lemon juice and whisk. Pour the dressing over the vegetables and mix until coated. Cover and refrigerate for 24 hours. Drain the marinade.

Preheat stovetop grill (or cast-iron skillet) to medium-high heat. Grill the vegetables for 6 to 8 minutes until lightly charred and cooked through. Transfer to a dish and keep warm.

ALMOND BUTTER Preheat oven to 300°F. Combine the ingredients in a bowl, toss, and then spread onto a baking sheet. Bake for 10 to 12 minutes, until the almonds are warmed through but without any colour.

Put the mixture in a blender and blend until smooth, adding more olive oil if needed. Transfer to a bowl and cool in the fridge.

TO ASSEMBLE Spread almond butter onto each toasted baguette slice, put on a large serving platter, and spoon over the warm Escalivada mixture, enough to cover each piece. Top with a draped slice of guanciale (or prosciutto), allowing the heat to slowly soften the fat of the cured meat.

TO SERVE Garnish the platter with chopped herbs, if using, and serve.

✛ Culmina Family Estate Winery | 2014 Grüner Veltliner | Oliver
Crisp citrus, dry, and richly textured with a long finish

Okanagan Fruit Sangria

Our sangria is just as popular as our martinis. We use dry wine, white or red, and we marinate the fruit for a day, so be sure to prepare it ahead of time. Unlike the traditional sangria, this version is topped with candied blackberries, which gives it a succulent, fresh sweetness. If you don't have blackberries handy, feel free to use blueberries or raspberries.

INGREDIENTS

1 medium lemon, halved

1 medium lime, halved

1 medium orange, halved

1 medium apple, cored and chopped

1 medium pear, cored and chopped

1 (750 mL) bottle dry Okanagan-style red or white wine

2 cups fruit nectar, such as peach, apricot, or pear

½ cup brandy

Splash of ginger ale, to serve

Candied Blackberries (recipe here), to serve

CANDIED BLACKBERRIES

1 cup blackberries

1 cup granulated sugar

1 cup boiling water

Serves 6 to 8

FIRST Combine the fruits, wine, fruit nectar, and brandy in a large covered container and mix well. Chill in the fridge for at least 24 hours. Strain into a pitcher and discard fruit. Refrigerate until use.

CANDIED BLACKBERRIES Combine blackberries and sugar in a bowl, pour boiling water overtop, and let sit until cooled. Put in the fridge for 30 minutes, until chilled.

TO SERVE Fill a tall glass with ice, and pour in enough sangria to fill three-quarters full. Top with ginger ale and garnish with a spoonful of candied blackberries.

Conversion Charts

VOLUME

IMPERIAL	METRIC
⅛ tsp	0.5 ml
¼ tsp	1 ml
½ tsp	2.5 ml
¾ tsp	4 ml
1 tsp	5 ml
½ Tbsp	8 ml
1 Tbsp	15 ml
1½ Tbsp	23 ml
2 Tbsp	30 ml
¼ cup	60 ml
⅓ cup	80 ml
½ cup	125 ml
⅔ cup	165 ml
¾ cup	185 ml
1 cup	250 ml
1¼ cups	310 ml
1⅓ cups	330 ml
1½ cups	375 ml
1⅔ cups	415 ml
1¾ cups	435 ml
2 cups	500 ml
2¼ cups	560 ml
2⅓ cups	580 ml
2½ cups	625 ml
2¾ cups	690 ml
3 cups	750 ml
4 cups/1 qt	1 L
5 cups	1.25 L
6 cups	1.5 L
7 cups	1.75 L
8 cups	2 L

WEIGHT

IMPERIAL	METRIC
½ oz	15 g
1 oz	30 g
2 oz	60 g
3 oz	85 g
4 oz (¼ lb)	115 g
5 oz	140 g
6 oz	170 g
7 oz	200 g
8 oz (½ lb)	225 g
9 oz	255 g
10 oz	285 g
11 oz	310 g
12 oz (¾ lb)	340 g
13 oz	370 g
14 oz	400 g
15 oz	425 g
16 oz (1 lb)	450 g
1¼ lb	570 g
1½ lb	670 g
2 lb	900 g
3 lb	1.4 kg
4 lb	1.8 kg
5 lb	2.3 kg
6 lb	2.7 kg

LIQUID MEASURES

IMPERIAL	METRIC
1 fl oz	30 ml
2 fl oz	60 ml
3 fl oz	90 ml
4 fl oz	120 ml

LINEAR

IMPERIAL	METRIC
⅛ inch	3 mm
¼ inch	6 mm
½ inch	12 mm
¾ inch	2 cm
1 inch	2.5 cm
1¼ inches	3 cm
1½ inches	3.5 cm
1¾ inches	4.5 cm
2 inches	5 cm
2½ inches	6.5 cm
3 inches	7.5 cm
4 inches	10 cm
5 inches	12.5 cm
6 inches	15 cm
7 inches	18 cm
10 inches	25 cm
12 inches	30 cm
13 inches	33 cm
16 inches	41 cm
18 inches	46 cm

BAKING PANS

IMPERIAL	METRIC
5- × 9-inch loaf pan	2 L loaf pan
9- × 13-inch cake pan	4 L cake pan
13- × 18-inch baking sheet	33- × 46-cm baking sheet

CANS & JARS

IMPERIAL	METRIC
14 oz	398 ml
28 oz	796 ml

OVEN TEMPERATURE

IMPERIAL	METRIC
200°F	95°C
250°F	120°C
275°F	135°C
300°F	150°C
325°F	160°C
350°F	180°C
375°F	190°C
400°F	200°C
425°F	220°C
450°F	230°C

TEMPERATURE

IMPERIAL	METRIC
90°F	32°C
120°F	49°C
125°F	52°C
130°F	54°C
140°F	60°C
150°F	66°C
155°F	68°C
160°F	71°C
165°F	74°C
170°F	77°C
175°F	80°C
180°F	82°C
190°F	88°C
200°F	93°C
240°F	116°C
250°F	121°C
300°F	149°C
325°F	163°C
350°F	177°C
360°F	182°C
375°F	191°C

Resource List

FARMERS AND PRODUCE SUPPLIERS

Bellmann Specialty Produce   bellmannspecialtyproduce.com
Specialty vegetables

David O'Neil Farms   (250) 769-0930
Quince

Duggan Farms   (250) 766-2628
Asparagus

Everything Green Organics   Bonnie Casavant   everythinggreenokanagan.com
Heirloom tomatoes, vegetables, micro greens, herbs

Everything Wild   Scott Moran   (250) 681-3431
Wild mushrooms, wild foraged items

Fester's Organics   (250) 498-6520
Salad greens, micro greens, peppers, other vegetables

Green City Acres   greencityacres.com
Lettuces, other vegetables

Jackalope Farms   jackalopefarms.ca
Strawberries, blackberries

Kelowna Farmers' Market   kelownafarmersandcraftersmarket.com
Seasonal artisanal items

The Kelowna Packing House   bctreefruits.com
Apples, pears, peaches, apricots

Little Creek   littlecreekdressing.com
Greens, tomatoes

Medley Organics   (250) 689-0848
Summer vegetables, root vegetables

Mikuni Wild Harvest   mikuniwildharvest.com
Black garlic, wild greens, fiddleheads, wild mushrooms

Old Meadows Organic Farm   oldmeadowsorganics.com
Corn, tomatoes, summer vegetables

Quail Hollow Farm   (250) 764-2321
Apples, Italian prune plums

Second Wind Farms   secondwindfarms.ca
Raspberries, flowers, vegetables

Stoney Paradise Farms   (604) 366-9290
Tomatoes, grapes, beans, onions

Suncatcher Farm   (250) 801-2843
Carrots, cauliflower, Romanesco broccoli, other vegetables

Sunshine Farm   sunshinefarm.net
Heirloom vegetables and seeds

What the Fungus   wtfmushrooms.ca
Assorted locally grown mushrooms

Wise Earth Farm   wiseearthfarm.com
Shallots, garlic, radishes, other vegetables

MEAT AND FISH SUPPLIERS

63 Acres Beef   63acresbeef.com
Beef

1846 BC Beef   1846.ca
Beef

Cache Creek Natural Beef Co.   cachecreeknaturalbeef.com
Beef

Canards du Lac Brome/Brome Lake Ducks   canardsdulacbrome.com
Duck breasts, duck legs, duck fat

Codfathers Seafood Market   codfathersseafoodmarket.com
Pacific fish and shellfish

Double R Ranch   snakeriverfarms.com/northwest-beef.html
Beef

Gordon Food Service B.C.   gfs.ca
B.C. beef, local cheese, B.C. produce

Harmony Farm   harmonyfarmkennelandlamb.com
Lamb

Helmut's Sausage   helmutssausagekitchen.ca
Lamb, prosciutto, salamis, sausage

Illichmann's Meats, Sausages & Gourmet Foods   illichmanns.com
Pork, lamb, sausages, cured meats

Lakeview Market   lakeview-market.com
Oxtail, pork, offcuts, breads, vegetables

North Okanagan Game Meats   (250) 838-7980
Venison, chicken, wild boar

Sedo's Old Fashioned Butcher and Deli   sedosbutchershop.com
Tyrolean-style cured bacon, charcuterie

Sterling Springs Chicken   sterlingspringschicken.com
Chicken, pepperoni, sausages

Sysco Kelowna   syscokelowna.ca
B.C. beef, international cheese, local produce

Two Rivers Specialty Meats   tworiversmeats.com
Turkey wings, B.C. beef, lamb, pork, charcuterie, offal, bison

Wild Moon Organics   wildmoon.org
Heritage pork

BREAD SUPPLIERS

Bread Co.   thebreadcompany.ca
Handmade bread items, sourdough, brioche

Okanagan Grocery   okanagangrocery.com
Artisanal organic bread items, baguettes, potato buns

DAIRY/CHEESE SUPPLIERS

Bella Stella Cheese   bellastellacheese.com
Ricotta

Blackwell Dairy Farm   blackwelldairy.com
Cream, milk, sour cream

Grass Root Dairies   gortsgoudacheese.bc.ca
Quark, gouda

Happy Days Dairy   happydaysdairy.com
Goat feta, goat chèvre

Kootenay Alpine Cheese Co.   kootenaymeadows.com
Nostrala, Alpindon

Little Qualicum Cheeseworks   cheeseworks.ca
Bleu Claire, Island Brie

Natural Pastures Cheese   naturalpastures.com
Comox brie, Buffalo brie, Boerenkaas

Poplar Grove Cheese   poplargrovecheese.ca
Double-cream camembert, Harvest Moon, Tiger Blue

Salt Spring Island Cheese   saltspringcheese.com
Chèvre, White Juliette, Blue Juliette, Romelia

Terroir Cheese   terroircheese.wordpress.com
Continental blue, Gruyère, Mont Ida

Upper Bench Creamery   upperbench.ca
King Cole, Gold, Grey Baby

Village Cheese Company   villagecheese.com
Aged Cheddar, smoked Cheddar, curds

PASTRY SUPPLIERS

Cacao Barry   cacao-barry.com
Chocolates, specialty pastry items

Whisk Cake Company   whiskcakes.com
Pastry and baking products

OTHER SUPPLIERS

Arlo's Honey Farm   arloshoneyfarm.com
Honey, raspberries, vegetables

Bean Scene Coffee Works   beanscene.ca
Roasted organic coffee

Brainy Bee Okanagan Honey   brainybee.ca
Honey

Three Farmers   threefarmers.ca
Camelina oil

Salt Spring Kitchen Co.   saltspringkitchen.com
Handcrafted jams

Silk Road Tea   silkroadteastore.com
Organic fresh teas

Valoroso Foods   valorosofoods.com
Pancetta, Parmesan, olives, international cheeses, carnaroli rice

The Vinegar Lady   thevinegarlady.com
Fruit vinegars

BREWERIES

Bad Tattoo Brewing Company   badtattoobrewing.com

BNA Brewing Co.   bnabrewing.com

Cannery Brewing   cannerybrewing.com

Crannóg Ales   crannogales.com

Driftwood Brewery   driftwoodbeer.com

Four Winds Brewing Company   fourwindsbrewing.ca

Hoyne Brewing Co.   hoynebrewing.ca

Kettle River Brewing Co.   kettleriverbrewing.ca

Persephone Brewing Company   persephonebrewing.com

Phillips Brewing and Malting Co.   phillipsbeer.com

Postmark Brewing   postmarkbrewing.com

Red Collar Brewing Co.   redcollar.ca

Steamworks Brewery   steamworks.com

Steel & Oak Brewing Co.   steelandoak.ca

Tree Brewery   treebeer.com

WINERIES

50th Parallel Estate   50thparallel.com

Andrew Peller Ltd.   andrewpeller.com

Arrowleaf Cellars   arrowleafcellars.com

Blue Mountain Vineyard and Cellars   bluemountainwinery.com

Burrowing Owl Estate Winery   bovwine.ca

C.C. Jentsch Cellars   ccjentschcellars.com

CedarCreek Estate Winery   cedarcreek.bc.ca

Checkmate Artisanal Winery   checkmatewinery.com

Church & State Wines   churchandstatewines.com

Coolshanagh Wines   coolshanagh.ca

Covert Farms Family Estate   covertfarms.ca/#organicfarmandwinery

Culmina Family Estate Winery   culmina.ca

Deep Roots Winery   deeprootswinery.com

Dirty Laundry Vineyard   dirtylaundry.ca

Gehringer Brothers Estate Winery   gehringerwines.ca

Gray Monk Estate Winery   graymonk.com

the hatch   thehatchwines.com

Haywire Winery at Okanagan Crush Pad   okanagancrushpad.com

Hester Creek Estate Winery   hestercreek.com

Intrigue Wines   intriguewines.ca

Kalala Organic Estate Winery   kalala.ca

Kettle Valley Winery   kettlevalleywinery.com

La Frenz Winery   lafrenzwinery.com

Lake Breeze Vineyards   lakebreeze.ca

Laughing Stock Vineyards   laughingstock.ca

Le Vieux Pin Winery   levieuxpin.ca

Liquidity Wines   liquiditywines.com

Meyer Family Vineyards   mfvwines.com

Mission Hill Family Estate   missionhillwinery.com

Moon Curser Vineyards   mooncurser.com

Moraine Estate Winery   morainewinery.com

Mt. Boucherie Estate Winery   mtboucheriewinery.com

Nagging Doubt Winery   naggingdoubt.com

Orofino Winery   orofinovineyards.com

Painted Rock Estate Winery   paintedrock.ca

Pentâge Winery   pentage.com

Quails' Gate Winery   quailsgate.com

Red Rooster Winery   redroosterwinery.com

River Stone Estate Winery   riverstoneestatewinery.ca

Road 13 Vineyards   road13vineyards.com

Sandhill Wines   sandhillwines.ca

Silkscarf Winery   silkw.net

SpierHead Winery   spierheadwinery.com

Stoneboat Vineyards   stoneboatvineyards.com

Tantalus Vineyards   tantalus.ca

Terravista Vineyards   terravistavineyards.com

TH Wines   thwines.com

Township 7 Vineyards & Winery   township7.com

Upper Bench Estate Winery   upperbench.ca

The View Winery & Vineyard   theviewwinery.com

vinAmité Cellars   vinamitecellars.com

Volcanic Hills Estate Winery   volcanichillswinery.com

The Young & Wyse Collection   youngandwysewine.com

DISTILLERIES

Dubh Glas Distillery   thedubhglasdistillery.com

Legend Distilling   legenddistilling.com

Long Table Distillery   longtabledistillery.com

Odd Society Spirits   oddsocietyspirits.com

Okanagan Spirits Craft Distillery   okanaganspirits.com

Old Order Distilling   oldorderdistilling.ca

Sheringham Distillery   sheringhamdistillery.com

Index

Acknowledgments

CHEFS MAKE LISTS. It's what we do every day. It's part of our DNA. But as I began to make the list of people to thank for bringing this project to life, I soon realized it would be much too long. Where to begin, and where would it stop? There are endless people throughout my career and life who have inspired me to get to this point. The team that supports me each day, and the individuals outside of work who continue to enrich my life, have all contributed in some significant way. So instead of a list, I will simply say: "From my heart I thank each of you. May your table always be surrounded with laughter and love, and may it be blessed with the earth's bounty."

Chef **ROD BUTTERS** has been committed to serving regional cuisine since long before "farm-to-table" and "organics" became part of the pop culture lexicon. After a storied career cooking for some of the world's top establishments, he settled in the Okanagan Valley in 2001, where he opened his first restaurant in the region, Fresco. He refers to the region as "the ultimate chef's playground" for its richness in agriculture and the passion of its farmers and wine producers. Rod is a member of the British Columbia Restaurant Hall of Fame and the Canadian Culinary Federation Honour Society, and an Honorary Fellow of Okanagan College. Butters's company RauDZ Creative Concepts Ltd. currently operates RauDZ Regional Table and micro bar • bites, both located in downtown Kelowna, B.C., and Terrafina at Hester Creek Estate Winery in Oliver, B.C.

Kelowna-based filmmaker and photographer **DAVID MCILVRIDE** first picked up a camera in the 1960s, shooting black-and-white photographs for a local newspaper in Ontario. In those early years working as a news photographer, McIlvride's lens captured photos of everyday people and a few icons, too, including Pierre Trudeau and Queen Elizabeth. He went on to produce social documentaries for major networks, including the Discovery Channel, CBC, National Geographic, and Channel 4 in the U.K. Today, McIlvride focuses on character studies and food as his subjects. His respect for the work and talents of chefs like Rod Butters is what drives his photography today.